THE MUMMY

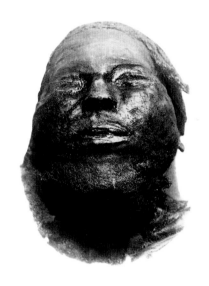

THIS IS A CARLTON BOOK

Text copyright © Joyce Tyldesley 1999
Design copyright © Carlton Books Limited, 1999

This edition published by
Carlton Books Limited, 1999

A CIP catalogue record for this book is
available from the British Library

ISBN 1-85868-771-3

Executive Editor: Sarah Larter
Project art direction: Adam Wright
Designer: Mary Ryan
Editor: Caroline Fraser Ker
Production: Alexia Turner
Picture Research: Alex Pepper

Printed and bound in Dubai

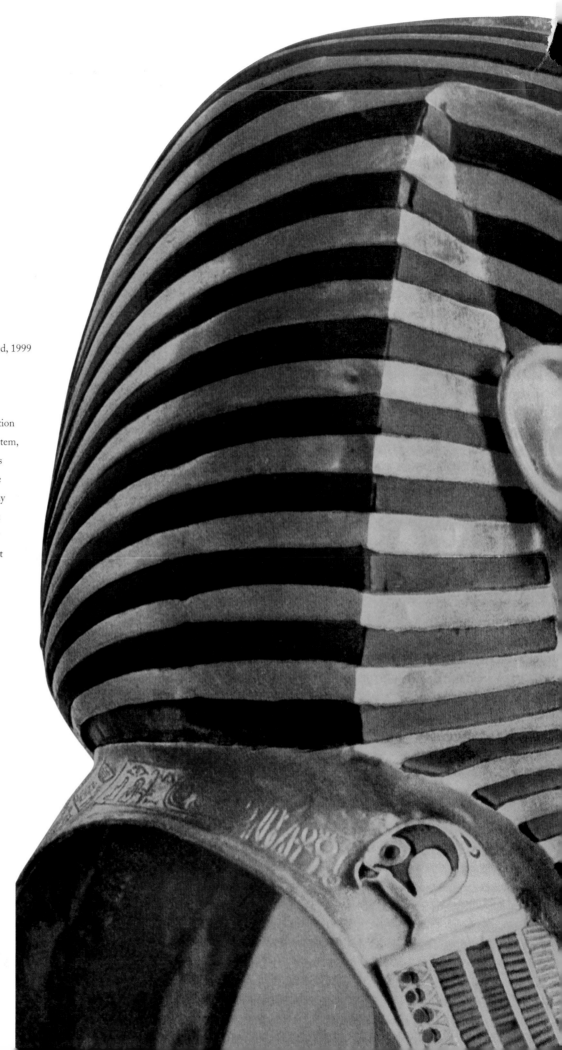

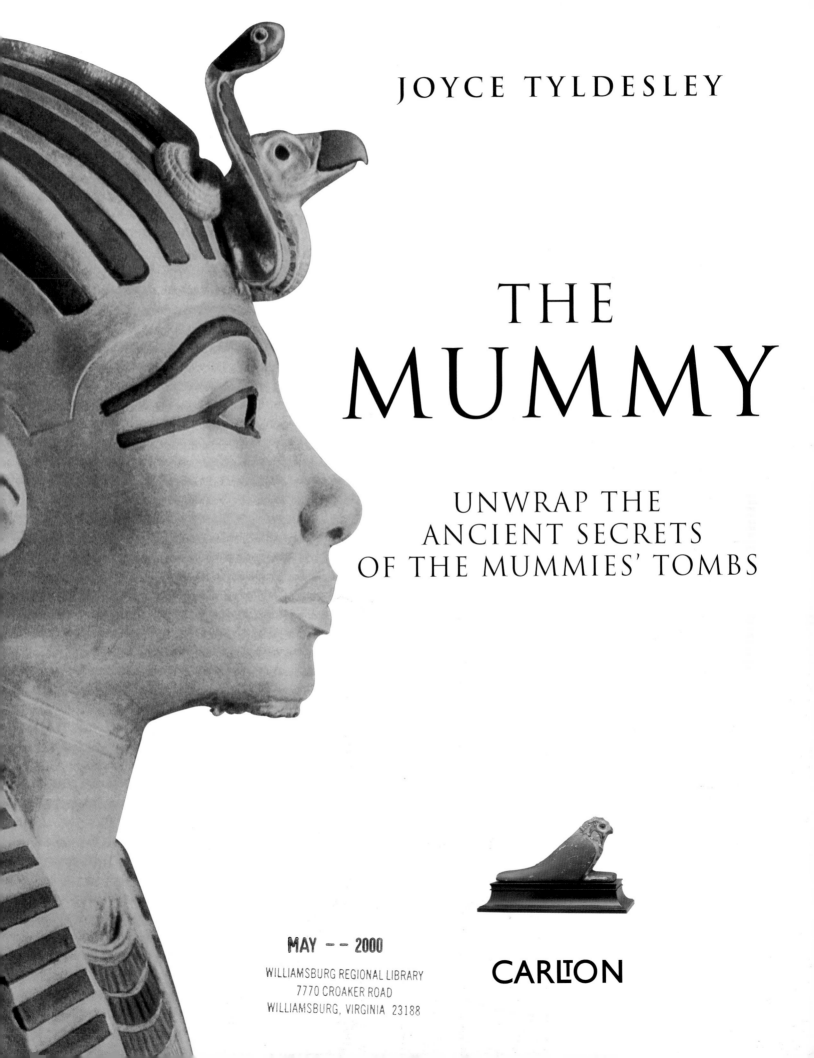

JOYCE TYLDESLEY

THE
MUMMY

UNWRAP THE
ANCIENT SECRETS
OF THE MUMMIES' TOMBS

CARLTON

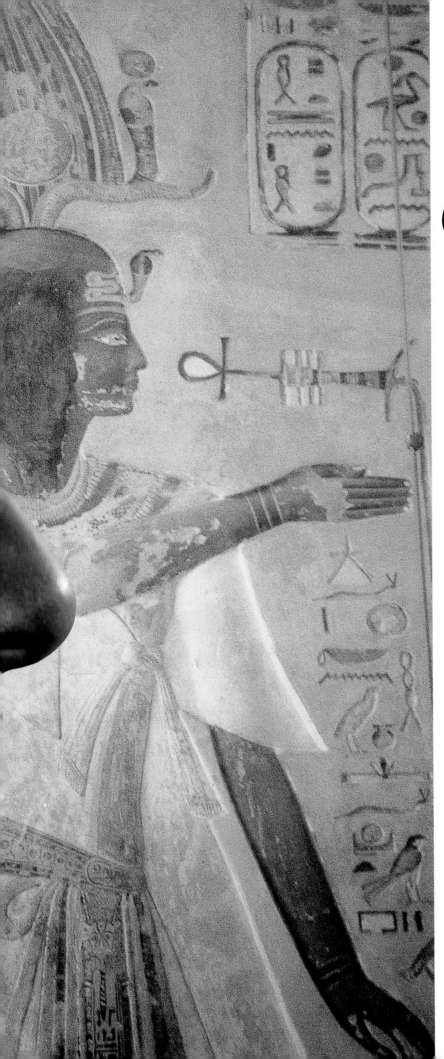

Contents

the SECOND DEATH

The Death of Osiris

Long ago, in the days when the gods ruled Egypt, the sky goddess Nut gave birth to four divine children. Osiris, Isis and Nephthys were born beautiful, wise and pure, but their brother Seth was marred by an infinite capacity for evil.

Osiris was destined to sit on the throne of the pharaohs. With his sister-wife Isis by his side Osiris reigned over Egypt for many peaceful years, proving himself a just and wise ruler, much loved by his people. This angered Seth who, growing increasingly jealous of his brother's success, resolved to murder the king and rule in his place.

Seth constructed a magnificent inlaid chest built to his brother's exact measurements. Then he threw a sumptuous banquet. Seth offered his chest as a prize to whoever could fit into it; all were eager to try, but only Osiris was successful. As soon as Osiris lay in the chest Seth slammed the lid shut. The chest, now a coffin, was locked, sealed in lead and thrown into the River Nile. Seth was able to proclaim himself king and Egypt was forced to bow before her new ruler.

ABOVE: THE RIVER NILE; THE BACKBONE OF EGYPT.

LEFT: OSIRIS, GOD OF THE AFTERLIFE, SHOWN AS A KING WRAPPED FOR BURIAL.

The coffin floated down the Nile and, after a violent storm, was washed up on the shore of Byblos. Here it became entangled in the branches of a great tree which slowly grew to enclose the coffin. In the fullness of time the tree was cut down and used as a pillar in the palace of the king.

Isis, mourning the loss of her husband, searched high and low for his body. Eventually she arrived in Byblos where, with the help of the queen, she was able to cut open the pillar and release Osiris. Isis returned to Egypt to bury her husband, hiding his body in the marsh. Unfortunately Seth discovered the body and dismembered it, scattering the fourteen pieces throughout the world.

Isis enlisted the help of Nephthys. Transforming themselves into giant birds, the two sisters searched high and low, retrieving Osiris' body parts and returning them to Egypt. Only his penis was missing; this had been eaten by the hungry Nile fish. Undaunted, Isis fashioned him a replica before reciting the sacred spell that would bring her husband back to life. So effective was her magic that Isis was soon pregnant with a son. Horus, son of Osiris, grew up to avenge his father. Deposing his treacherous uncle he took his rightful place on the throne of Egypt. Meanwhile, Osiris continued to rule over his own shadowy land, the Kingdom of the Dead.

Thus the story of Osiris offered hope of a life beyond death. From this time onwards the living king of Egypt was identified with Horus; dead kings became one with Osiris.

RIGHT: OSIRIS, SUPPORTED BY HIS SISTER-WIFE THE GODDESS ISIS AND HIS SON THE FALCON-HEADED GOD HORUS.

ABOVE: THE MARSH LANDS BORDERING THE RIVER NILE TEEMED WITH WILDLIFE.

The Egyptian galleries of our national museums are all too often dark and gloomy places, crammed with objects associated with the rituals of death. The abundance of funeral furniture, grave goods, painted coffins and, of course, the imposing presence of the elaborately bandaged corpses themselves, suggests that the ancient Egyptians were an unhealthily morbid race, obsessed with thoughts of their own mortality. In fact, nothing could be further from the truth. The Egyptians were a vibrant, happy people who loved life so much that they resolved to cling on to it beyond the grave.

The gods had smiled on Egypt, endowing her with abundant natural resources. The climate was invariably sunny and warm, with little or no rain. The River Nile, Egypt's natural highway, provided irrigation for fields so fertile that seed sown in the November spring could be guaranteed to yield a magnificent harvest of vegetables, fruit and grain.

Fish, fowl, bread and beer were freely available to all, while a lucky few enjoyed sumptuous banquets of meat and cakes washed down with wine. The papyrus plants that fringed the Nile could be pressed to make paper, flax could be woven into white linen cloth, and even the thick Nile mud was a gift from the gods; not only did it allow the villagers to make their own simple pottery, compressed and moulded into bricks, it also made a cheap and convenient building material. Beyond the fertile soil lay the desert and the mountains which yielded gold, semi-precious gems and the stone needed for monumental building.

However, Egypt was a land of stark contrasts. The precious fertile soil lining the banks of the Nile was itself bordered by arid sand. The difference between the cultivation or "Black Land" and the desert or "Red Land" was so immediate and so extreme that it shocked visitors to Egypt.

Throughout the dynastic age it was possible to stand astride the boundary with one foot on the soil and one foot on the sand. Here, in the absence of water, nothing would grow and no one could live. Only the dead could make use of the Red Land and so the desert became reserved for the architecture of death; elaborate tombs, mortuary temples and simple pit graves. The West, land of the setting sun, had became the land of the dead. This juxtaposition of the fertile and the barren, light and dark, the living and the dead, served as an ever-present reminder of man's mortality.

Just as the Egyptian night fell swiftly, so death could strike at any moment. Life expectancy at birth was less than twenty years, while those who survived the perils of infancy and childhood might look forward to a further two decades.

The skill of the Egyptian physicians was famed throughout the Mediterranean world but they had little understanding of the workings of the human body and no idea how to control the diseases which plagued the population. When faced with a sick child they could do little to avert disaster. Polio, measles, diarrhoea and even a severe cold could, and often did, prove fatal. Childbirth, a yearly hazard for most married women, killed many mothers and their babies, while Egypt's quarries, building sites, mines and battlefields provided hazardous working conditions for men. Occasional natural disasters, floods, such as fires and famines, contributed to the death toll.

Barring accidents and battles, ancient Egyptians were born and died at home, nursed by their family and friends. This meant that no one could hope to avoid contact with the dying or the recently dead. Death was a fact of everyday life. But, if death was a frequent visitor, it was never a welcome one. The gravestone of the Lady Taimhotep laments the cruel fate which snatched a mother away from her family:

… The West is a land of sleep where darkness weighs on the dwelling place. Those who live there sleep as mummies. They do not wake to see their brothers and cannot see their fathers or mothers. Their hearts forget their wives and children … turn my face to the north wind at the edge of the water. Perhaps then my heart will be cooled in its grief.

Recognizing that it made little sense to plan for old age, the ancient Egyptians spent their earthly years planning for life beyond death.

Egyptian theology taught that the death of the body was not necessarily the end of life. This was not a particularly unusual belief. Many societies, ancient and modern, have clung to the hope that the soul or spirit can survive beyond the grave. Most cultures, however, see the soul as one entity; the single essence of the dead person. The Egyptians believed that the soul was represented by three different spiritual forms, each of which had its own limitations, possibilities and requirements, and each of which had to survive to ensure eternal life. These three spirits, the Ba, the Ka and the Akh, would be set free at the moment of death.

The Ba, visualized as a human-headed bird, represented the personality, character or individuality of the deceased. The Ba dwelt in the tomb but was free to come and go as it wished and often visited the land of the living where it could assume any form.

In contrast the Ka, or spirit of life, had a more limited existence. Fashioned by the creator god Khnum at the time of conception, the Ka was an exact physical and emotional replica of the deceased imprisoned within the living heart. Expelled by death, the Ka was compelled to remain at all times close to the body and could never leave the confines of the grave. As the Ka could not survive without nourishment – it required food, drink and even clothing – it fell to the friends and family of the deceased to leave regular offerings at the tomb.

The third spirit, the Akh, represented the immortality of the deceased. This spirit was free to leave the tomb and shine among the stars in the night sky, sail by day in the solar

LEFT: THE HUMAN-HEADED BA BIRD.

BELOW: THE RAISED ARMS ON THE HEAD OF THIS STATUE REPRESENT THE KA OF THE DEAD KING.

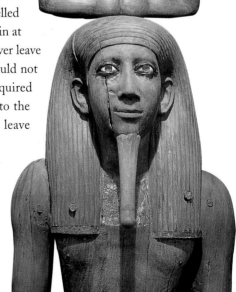

boat of the sun-god Re, or dwell forever with King Osiris in the Field of Reeds.

The Field of Reeds, or Field of Offerings, was a wonderful place – the direct parallel of the living world ruled by a dead rather than a living king. Here all the best aspects of Egyptian life were magnified many times – there was a cool flowing river, fertile fields, abundant crops and fat cattle. There were no floods, famines, pests or diseases to

ABOVE: A PAGE FROM *THE CHAPTERS OF COMING FORTH BY DAY* BELONGING TO THE DECEASED ANI.

disturb the tranquillity. And, best of all, an army of servants was provided to perform all necessary manual labour. Reunited with their loved ones, the deceased, now permanently restored to health and vigour, could spend all eternity eating, drinking and relaxing in a land of pleasure and plenty.

The delights of the Afterlife could never be taken for granted. Originally the Kingdom of Osiris had been exclusively reserved for dead pharaohs. Mere commoners had been condemned to pass a dreary Afterlife perpetually haunting their own grave. It was as a response to this harsh theology that Egypt's elite started to build the largest and most comfortable tombs that money could buy. In time the rule was relaxed so that by the New Kingdom everyone was, in theory, enti-tled to dwell with Osiris. However not everyone was accepted into the Kingdom. A devout or virtuous earthly life, although an admirable achievement, did nothing to guarantee admission

to the Egyptian heaven. Entrance to this most exclusive of clubs was by examination only.

After death, the Akh would embark on a long and perilous journey passing over the western horizon to reach a labyrinth of gates and doors. Here it would face a relentless cross-questioning from both the door-keepers and the magical doors themselves. It was considered essential that the spirit could address the tormenters by name, as knowledge of a personal name was believed to confer power over an individual:

> *"I will not let you enter through me", says the jamb of the door, "unless you tell me my name."*
> *"Plumb-bob in the Place of Truth is your name".*
> *"I will not open for you", says the bolt of the door, "unless you tell me my name".*
> *"Toe of his Mother is your name."*

Those with a bad memory had no need to worry. Prudent Egyptians ensured that they were buried with complete sets of questions and answers which would enable them to pass the interrogation with flying colours. The Old Kingdom pharaohs were provided with the *Pyramid Texts*, a series of spells devized to protect the dead king, enabling him to fulfil his ultimate destiny of eternal life. During the Middle Kingdom the common man's guide to the Afterlife took the form of spells and incantations. The *Coffin Texts* could not be forgotten. They were, as their name suggests, conveniently painted on the side of the coffin. In the New Kingdom a papyrus scroll, inscribed with *The Chapters of Coming Forth by Day*, now univer-sally known as *The Book of the Dead*, guaranteed examination success.

Passing through the labyrinth the spirit would reach the hall of judgement where the forty-two assessor-gods sat on the divine tribunal. Here, before Osiris, the deceased was expected to make a series of pre-prepared speeches justifying his or her earthly existence. The emphasis was on the avoidance of sin, rather than the active pursuit of a good life, and there was no need to apologize for any lapses from virtue – spells intended to protect the dead from the consequences of their earthly misdeeds ensured that few had cause to worry:

I have not acted evilly towards anyone …
I have not committed sins … I have not
reviled the gods … I have not stolen the
cakes of the blessed … I have not copulated
unlawfully, or indulged in fornication.

As a dramatic climax the jackal-headed god Anubis would weigh the heart of the deceased against a feather symbolizing truth and justice. Thoth, the scribe of the gods, would record the result in his scroll. Only the true in heart would pass this test. The hearts of those who failed were fed to Ammit, "Eater of the Dead", an awe-inspiring monster with the head of a crocodile, foreparts of a lion and hindquarters of a hippopotamus. Those eaten by Ammit were doomed to haunt the living as evil spirits. Those who succeeded before the tribunal were granted a plot of land in the Field of Reeds. Here they could relax safe from all harm.

However, there was still one potential cloud on the horizon. If it was possible to live again, logic dictated that it had to be possible to die again. Dying the Second Death, the permanent obliteration of the spirit from which there could be no possible return, was the worst fate that an Egyptian could envisage. Spells "for not perishing in the land of the dead" were included in tombs from a very early date.

The Second Death was caused by the loss of all earthly memory of the deceased. In practice, this meant the destruction of the corpse. In order to survive the Ka needed to be able to return to its physical host. If the body decayed beyond recognition the Ka too would perish, and the death of this one aspect of the soul would lead to the destruction of both the Ba and the Akh. In an emergency the Ka could take up residence in a statue of the deceased or in an image on the tomb wall. Even the remembrance of the name of the departed offered some hope of eternal life, and so we find successive pharaohs filling Egypt with portrait-statues and inscriptions in a desperate attempt to ensure that their name would live forever. They knew that once they were forgotten by the living they would die among the dead.

The Egyptians were practical people. Having decided that the body must survive in a recognizable form beyond death, they set out to ensure that it would. So started centuries of experimentation. The science of mummification – artificially preserving the corpses of the dead – had been born.

BELOW: DIVINE JUDGEMENT: THOTH WEIGHS THE HEART OF ANI IN THE COURT OF OSIRIS. AMMIT "EATER OF THE DEAD" LOOKS ON.

the ART *of* EMBALMING

1

Thousands of years ago, long before the dawn of the dynastic age, the prehistoric Egyptians buried their dead in shallow, oval pits dug into the hot desert sands. Even at this early date there was a hope that life could continue beyond death, and the deceased were provided with items which they might find useful or ornamental in their new home. Stout storage vessels housed the food and drink which would be needed on the long journey ahead, while more personal items, stone tools, bone combs, decorated pots and bead jewellery, hint at the expectation of an Afterlife similar to mortal life in the Nile Valley.

Within these early graves the dead lay as if sleeping, curled into the fetal position with the knees drawn up to the chest and the hands held before the face. Often the bodies lay on their left side with the head pointing south and the face looking towards the setting sun. No coffins were used in these simple pits; the body was merely wrapped in woven matting or animal skins, placed in a hole and covered with sand. There was therefore no physical barrier, and most importantly no air, separating the corpse from the desert which now entombed it. These particular conditions had a remarkable effect on the preservation of the bodies within the graves.

LEFT AND ABOVE: THE JACKAL-HEADED GOD ANUBIS ATTENDS TO THE MUMMY OF SENNEDJEM.

NATURAL MUMMIFICATION

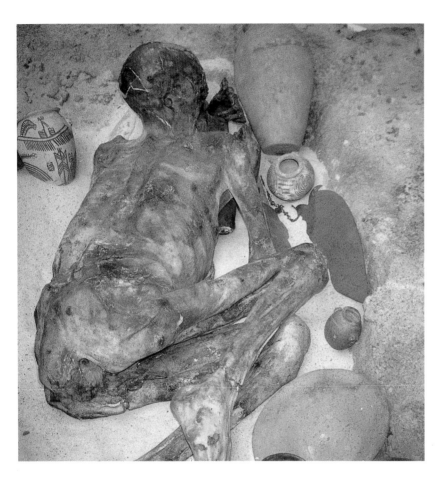

ABOVE: "GINGER", A NATURALLY DESICCATED PREHISTORIC BODY NOW HOUSED IN THE BRITISH MUSEUM, LONDON.

The human body, some 75 per cent by weight water, begins to decompose quickly after death, whatever the circumstances. Those internal organs which contain digestive enzymes start to self-destruct within a few hours, effectively eating themselves – a process known as autolysis. After this early stage the process of decomposition is influenced by external factors such as humidity and temperature. In a temperate environment putrefaction begins in about three days and then becomes progressive. Although the purifying bacteria largely originate in the intestine and lungs, the internal organs do not decompose more rapidly than the skin. After some months the soft tissues as a whole disintegrate leaving, eventually, the skeleton. If the body is buried soon after death the process of bacterial action may be slowed down

considerably. In some cases, however, drying out of the body occurs and putrefaction does not take place. The dryness of the surroundings is the significant factor; the bacterial growth is inhibited and the tissues simply lose water.

In Egypt's predynastic graves the hot sterile porous sand drew the body fluids away from the corpse, preventing the onset of decay. The bodies dried quickly and naturally with their internal organs, connective tissue, tendons and ligaments preserved. Their darkened skin, baked to a hard membrane, remained in place as did their hair and even their nails. When, as occasionally happened, an old grave was disturbed by animals or by later grave-diggers, its long-dead occupant was still recognizably human. This made it obvious to everyone that the preservation of the body beyond death was possible.

The simple pit graves were used by rich and poor alike for hundreds of years. Eventually, however, there came a natural desire to protect the bodies from the sand which totally enveloped them. This started in a modest way with upturned baskets placed over the faces of the deceased so that the sand would not clog their eyes and mouths. Pillows placed beneath the head ensured that the dead would rest in peace. Soon the upper classes abandoned the traditional skin and matting winding sheets in favour of basketwork trays or boxes placed above and below the corpse. The use of coffins – squat wooden boxes designed to hold the contracted burials – was a logical development, as was the provision of a wooden roof and a plaster or mud-brick lining which effectively converted the simple pit grave into a miniature tomb. Here Egypt's elite could lie in comfort without fear of contamination by a single grain of sand. Unfortunately this separation from the desert allowed nature to take her course. Cocooned within a coffin, sarcophagus and tomb, and surrounded by ever-increasing numbers of valuable objects, the upper classes started to rot in their graves.

PROBLEMS OF PUTREFACTION

It is ironic that those who struggled most to make adequate provision for the Afterlife were the least likely to survive to enjoy it. The poor, who through necessity continued with the tradition of simple pit graves, had no problem with decomposing corpses. The rich were now invariably reduced to skeletons within their stone tombs. For a people who believed that the entire body must be preserved to ensure the survival of the soul, this was a disaster. And yet no one wanted to return to the old ways of simple pit graves for all. If the Ka was to survive for all eternity entombed with the body, it surely needed a comfortable, well-appointed home where it could receive gifts of food and drink from the living. Furthermore, the new stone-lined tombs, dug deep beneath the desert sand, offered a degree of protection against the unscrupulous robbers who now preyed upon Egypt's cemeteries, attracted by the valuable grave goods contained inside.

If the increasingly elaborate funeral rituals were to be maintained, a means must be found of combatting decay. The search was on to find a way of cheating nature and conserving the body beyond death.

The Egyptians were not the only, or even the first, peoples of the ancient world to attempt the artificial preservation of the dead. Thousands of years earlier the hunter-gatherer Chinchorro people of northern Chile had developed an elaborate mortuary ritual which involved dismembering, skinning, defleshing, drying and reassembling the body. Chincorro mummification typically started with the beheading, dismemberment and skinning of the corpse. The body cavity was dried with hot coals and the brains extracted. The body was then reconstructed; sticks were inserted to provide much needed internal support, while the abdomen was stuffed with grass and ashes. The corpse was coated in a paste of wood ash, and the skin and hair stuck back in place. Maintained by annual coats of paint these gruesome relics were displayed on important ceremonial occasions.

However, it is the Egyptian method of embalming which has given rise to the term "mummification", a term which is now commonly used to describe both naturally and artificially preserved bodies from all over the world. The name itself is something of a historical accident. The first visitors to Egypt, observing that many of the embalmed bodies had been coated in a black, glossy resin, erroneously concluded that the ancients preserved their dead by dipping them in pitch or bitumen. The fact that the black mummies burned well – apparently giving out a great heat – seemed to support the assumption that they contained a high percentage of pitch. They therefore coined the word "mummy", derived from the Arabic word "*mummiya*" meaning bitumen or bitumenized.

LEFT: A STRIKING EXAMPLE OF A BITUMENIZED HUMAN HEAD.

EARLY MUMMIES AND ROTTING CORPSES

The first Egyptian attempts at mummification involved wrapping the semi-flexed corpse in many tight layers of bandages before placing it in a short wooden coffin. This was the technique used to preserve the body of Djer, one of the earliest kings of the dynastic age whose funeral took place in the Abydos cemetery some five thousand years ago. Although Djer's body had been ripped apart by tomb robbers the lower part of a single arm, bandaged in fine linen and still dressed with four bracelets beaded in gold, turquoise, lapis lazuli and amethyst, survived to be recovered by the English archaeologist Flinders Petrie. Djer's arm represented the earliest example of attempted

ABOVE:
FLINDERS PETRIE:
THE FATHER OF EGYPTIAN
ARCHAEOLOGY.

mummification but not everyone appreciated its importance; including M. Brugsch, curator of Cairo Museum, who threw away both the arm and its bandages.

The use of resin-soaked linen plus a judicious amount of padding under the bandages allowed the undertakers to mould the limbs, features, breasts and even genitals of the deceased into a parody of life. To enhance their appearance some early mummies were given painted green faces – green being the accepted colour of resurrection rather than putrefaction – while others were coated with a thin layer of plaster which allowed for a more delicate modelling of the face. Occasionally the mummy was dressed in a linen garment worn over the bandages. All this work was, however, entirely cosmetic. The embalmers appeared to be doing a good job, but inevitably, decay set in underneath the bandages. Before long, all that remained of these early mummies was a skeleton covered by a rigid linen shell whose blackened inner layers bore testimony to the heat generated by the decomposition of the flesh within.

EVISCERATION

It was soon recognized that if the body was to stand a chance of survival beneath its bandages the soft internal organs – in particular the liver, intestines and stomach – would have to be removed soon after death. This would delay the onset of putrefaction and allow a thorough drying of the emptied body cavity. The embalmers therefore started to slit open the abdomen, drawing out the organs before packing the dried cavity with resin-soaked linen and sealing the incision with yet more resin. It is probably no

coincidence that elongated rather than flexed burials now became fashionable among the upper classes; it must have been far easier for the undertakers to perform the rites on a straight body.

One of the earliest examples of an eviscerated mummy was that of the 4th Dynasty Ranefer, who was discovered lying in his Meydum tomb by Flinders Petrie in 1890. Ranefer's entrails, neatly wrapped, were stored in a niche within his tomb wall. His abdomen had been packed with resin-soaked linen while his linen-bound head, which had become detached when robbers seized his copper necklace, had been painted to give a semblance of life. Ranefer had journeyed to his

Afterlife with black hair, green eyes, green eyebrows and a red mouth. His separated head rattled when shaken; clear evidence that a shrivelled brain remained within the cranial cavity. Unfortunately Ranefer's body and head were destroyed during the Second World War bombing of London.

A second Meydum mummy, recovered in 1910, also showed signs of evisceration; in this case the body cavity had been stuffed with vegetation and the brain had been removed via the foramen magnum at the base of the skull. However, the bandages which bound this nameless mummy rested directly upon its bones, while the atlas vertebra at the neck, although correctly placed, was upside down. Clearly the body had been disrupted, and the flesh stripped from the bones, before the bandages were applied. Other examples of Old Kingdom mummy wrappings enclosing disarticulated bones were encountered at the Deshasha cemetery site.

This evidence, taken in conjunction with occasional finds of disarticulated predynastic burials, provoked lively debate among Egyptologists. Some argued that Egypt must have passed through an experimental phase of ritual de-fleshing, dismembering and even cannibalism which lasted from the prehistoric age until the end of the Old Kingdom. Others maintained that the Meydum body was an example of the secondary wrapping of a mummy which had been disturbed – possibly by tomb robbers – some time after its original burial. There was always the possibility that the body had decayed before it was submitted to the embalmers, or that it had met with an accident in the undertakers' workshop; X-ray analysis of later period mummies shows that the neatest bandages could conceal a jumbled mass of bones. Whatever the explanation, there is little evidence from later periods to suggest that defleshing ever became common practice. The Egyptians were intent on preserving the body intact, not destroying it. The magical *Pyramid Texts* summed up the position: "O flesh of the king, do not decay, do not rot, do not stink".

The organs extracted from the stomach could not be thrown away because, if all went according to plan, they would be needed in the Afterlife. There was, however, no reason why they should not be preserved and stored separately within the tomb, awaiting the moment when they would be magically reunited with their host body. At first, as in the case of Ranefer, the organs were simply dried, wrapped in linen and placed in a special niche in the tomb wall. Eventually special containers were developed; when rediscovered, the tomb of the 4th Dynasty Queen Hetepheres, mother of the pyramid-building King Khufu, included a simple alabaster casket which still held the remains of her viscera preserved in a salt solution. Soon even relatively humble burials were provided with jars to store the organs and wooden chests to hold the jars.

FURTHER DEVELOPMENTS

The earliest mummies, although eviscerated, still had a disturbing tendency to decay underneath their bandages. Consequently, few Old Kingdom mummies have survived the ravages of time. The embalmers, aware of their failures, experimented

BELOW: A BADLY PRESERVED MIDDLE KINGDOM FEMALE MUMMY.

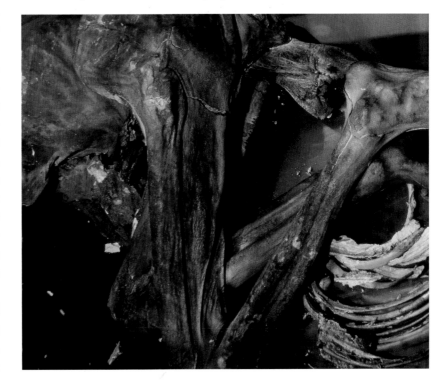

throughout the Middle Kingdom and their techniques continued to improve. The mummy of Wah, an 11th Dynasty Theban estate manager, is a good example of the technique used in the Middle Kingdom. Wah had escaped the clutches of tomb robbers, resting undisturbed in his grave. His intact mummy was unwrapped under scientific conditions at the Metropolitan Museum, New York, in 1935. The autopsy showed that Wah had died in his early thirties. He had been eviscerated via a slit in the abdomen, but his lungs and his brain had been left in place. His bandages had been carefully applied; when unrolled they yielded layers of padding, resin and a fine collection of jewellery and protective amulets. However someone in the embalmers' workshop had been careless: not only did the innermost bandages reveal the dirty fingerprints of the morticians, but wrapped inside the bandages were also the remains of a mouse, a lizard and a cricket.

Throughout the dynastic age mummified bodies were protected by a wooden coffin, which was itself loaded with religious symbolism. At first the

LEFT: AN ELABORATELY GILDED MUMMY CASE DATING TO THE GRAECO-ROMAN PERIOD.

RIGHT: A MIDDLE KINGDOM MUMMY IN ITS SIMPLE BOX COFFIN.

rectangular box-like coffin was viewed as an eternal home, like the tomb itself, and was therefore painted or carved to resemble a house. In the Middle Kingdom this decoration was further elaborated to included painted doors through which the Ka could come and go, sometimes surmounted by "magic eyes" which allowed the Ka to peer out from within the coffin.

The most important advance in coffin development was the evolution of the mummiform or anthropoid (person-shaped) coffin. This form of coffin was intended to make the deceased resemble the god Osiris – a mummiform king – as much as possible. To achieve the desired appearance the coffin was moulded into the curves of a mummy, often complete with a painted shroud and bandages, while the head was left uncovered to reveal a royal false beard and head-cloth. The face was sometimes painted black or green, like that of Osiris himself, to symbolize ideas of rebirth. These mummiform coffins continued in popularity for as long as the Egyptians mummified their dead. Today they provide one of the most immediately recognizable images of the idiosyncratic burial practices of the ancient Egyptians.

THE SACRED MYSTERIES

Between the 18th and the 21st Dynasties the embalmer's art, now some fifteen centuries old, reached its peak. Now it was perfectly possible to preserve a body for all time. Unfortunately for modern historians, the mysteries of mummification were never recorded in writing. Egypt's embalmers conducted their lucrative trade under a cloak of ritual secrecy, with techniques and methods being passed down from father to son. Rumours of awful, stomach-churning rituals within the embalmers' workshops fascinated foreign tourists, including the Greek historians Herodotus and Diodorus Siculus, who wrote about them with great gusto. It is from these accounts – written at the very end of the dynastic age, but based on traditional practices – that much of our understanding of the embalming process has been obtained.

We learn from Herodotus how the death of a family member would precipitate an uncontrollable outbreak of grief. The women of the household would plaster their heads and faces with dust to wander through the streets beating their bare breasts in anguish. The men, slightly more restrained, would tear their clothes and beat themselves. Then, with the public grieving temporarily halted, the corpse would be carried to the undertaker's office. Here the family would be shown wooden figurines or models – just as modern shoppers may be shown salesman's samples – designed to demonstrate the three styles of mummification on offer. The recommended, most expensive method was that which was believed to have been used to preserve the body of the great god Osiris:

… this is their procedure for the most perfect style of embalming. First of all they draw out the brain through the nostrils using an iron hook. When they have extracted all that they can, they wash out the remnants with an infusion of drugs. Then, using a sharp obsidian stone, they make a cut along the flank. Through this they extract the whole

ABOVE: A GROUP OF PROFESSIONAL FEMALE MOURNERS AT THE FUNERAL OF THE NOBLEMAN RAMOSE.

contents of the abdomen. The abdomen is then cleaned, rinsed with palm wine and rinsed again with powdered spices but not frankincense, and stitched up. And when they have done this they heap the body with natron for seventy days, but no longer, and so the mummy is made. After the seventy days are over they wash the body and wrap it from head to toe in the finest linen bandages coated with resin … Finally they hand back the body to the relatives who place it in a wooden coffin in the shape of a man before shutting it up in a tomb, propped upright against the wall.

Diodorus Siculus, writing four hundred years later, goes into greater detail. He tells us the cost of this elaborate ritual – an exorbitant one talent of silver – adding that some undertakers required advance payment. Then, after opening the abdomen:

... one of them inserts his hand through the wound in the body into the breast and takes out everything except the kidneys and the heart. Another man cleans each of the entrails, washing them with palm wine and with incense. Finally, having washed the whole corpse, they first diligently treat it with cedar oil and other things for thirty days, and then with myrrh, cinnamon and spices ... Having treated it they return it to the relatives with every member of the body preserved so perfectly that even the eyelashes and the eyebrows remain, the whole

BELOW: AN ELABORATE ALABASTER VESSEL FROM THE TOMB OF TUTANKHAMEN.

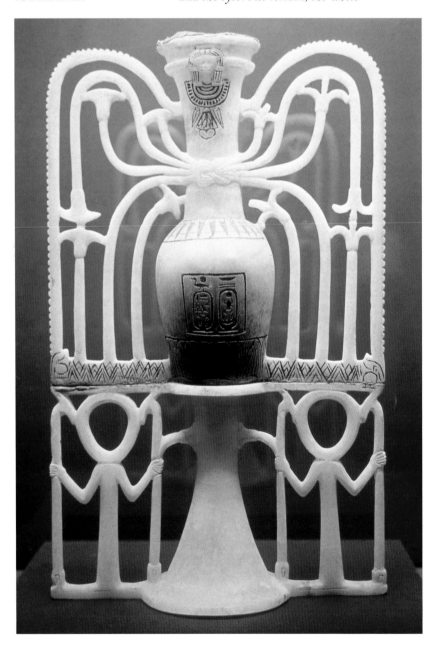

appearance of the body being unchanged and the cast of the features recognizable.

The second, less labour-intensive and less costly method of embalming required the undertaker to inject the corpse with oils applied via the rectum:

The embalmers fill their syringes with cedar oil which they inject into the abdomen. They do not cut the flesh or extract the internal organs, but introduce the oil through the anus which is then stopped up. Then they mummify the body for the prescribed number of days. After this they allow the oil which has been injected to escape. So great is its strength that it carries away all the internal organs in liquid form.

An external drying agent could then be used to draw moisture out of the corpse.

There is some evidence to suggest that the technique of evisceration by injection was practised during the Middle Kingdom. A group of mummified princesses recovered from the rock-cut tombs of Deir el-Bahari had all been dried, coated in resin and bandaged, yet none of them showed the tell-tale cut in the left flank. Their slightly dilated vaginas and rectums suggest that an attempt may have been made to remove the viscera by injection but, as their bodies still contained traces of shrivelled organs, they may simply have been mummified intact. Two Late Period mummies also lack the embalming scar, but again it may simply be that they were never eviscerated. Nature would ensure that the entrails of any corpse buried in natron would disintegrate to a brown sludge which would seep from the body. Herodotus is somewhat vague about the oil used in the injection – his "cedar oil" could perhaps be juniper oil – but it seems likely that any liquid enema would hasten the process of decomposition, just as water injected into the skull was useful for softening and flushing out the brain.

The third and cheapest method of embalming was reserved for the poor; "the undertakers clean out the abdomen with a purge, mummify the corpse for seven days, then give it back to be taken away".

 # HOW TO MAKE A MUMMY

Herodotus was very much the credulous tourist, believing everything that he was told by the locals. Nevertheless, it seems that there is a great deal of truth in his account of Egyptian mortuary practices. It is one of the often repeated fallacies which Egyptology seems to attract, that the secret of mummification died with the pharaohs. In fact we now have a good understanding of the methods used, derived from a mixture of ancient and modern sources. The reports of Herodotus and Diodorus Siculus plus other contemporary documentation have been combined with archaeological research, the scientific analysis of actual mummies, and modern experimentation with animal and occasionally human bodies to explain the process of embalming.

Soon after death, before the onset of putrefaction, the body was taken to the *Ibu*, the Place of Purification or Place of Washing. Here it was stripped and cleaned in Nile water mixed with natron – a ritual act intended to symbolize the rebirth of the dead. The *Ibu* was, for reasons of both hygiene and secrecy, situated in the Red Land close to the cemetery and with easy access to water.

ABOVE: DURING THE FUNERAL THE MUMMIFORM COFFIN WAS THE FOCUS OF CEREMONIES INTENDED TO RESTORE LIFE TO THE DECEASED.

ABOVE: THE FIGURE OF ANUBIS ON THE HANDLE OF THIS KNIFE SUGGESTS THAT IT WAS POSSIBLY USED DURING THE PROCESS OF MUMMIFICATION.

No one in his right mind would have chosen to live close to an Egyptian charnel house. Egypt is a hot country and the conditions, smells and of course flies within the mortuary complex would have been enough to turn even the strongest stomach. Good ventilation would have been essential; it is possible that all the mortuary rituals were conducted in tents rather than in walled buildings. Unfortunately, open-sided tents would attract desert scavengers, intent on snatching a highly salted meal. It may therefore have proved necessary to mount a constant guard over the bodies.

Occasionally there might be a deliberate delay in submitting the body to the *Ibu*. Herodotus, never averse to a bit of gossip, reports that it was customary for the bodies of rich or attractive women to be withheld for a few days: "They do this to prevent the undertakers violating the corpse. For it is rumoured that one of them was caught who had actually abused a freshly-dead woman; a work-mate denounced him". Certainly, it is true that many Later Period mummies suffered decomposition and fly infestation beneath their bandages – a sure sign that they were not mummified immediately after death – however this condition applied equally to both male and female mummies.

The purified corpse was transferred to the nearby *Per-Nefer*, the House of Mummification. Here it lay extended on four wooden blocks resting upon a wooden table. The removal of the soft tissue began with the extraction of the brain, which was a delicate and awkward operation, only assisted by

the semi-liquid consistency of the cranial tissue after death. A small chisel, inserted via the nostril, was used to break the fragile ethmoid bone, pushing it up into the cranial cavity. This allowed the insertion of a hook or an iron rod, again through the nostril, to draw down fragments of cerebral matter.

Fragments could be scooped out with a long-handled spoon, while canny undertakers filled the skull with water to encourage the decomposition of the remaining brain. The head could then be propped upright, allowing the now-liquid brain to drain out through the nose. As the function and importance of the brain was still not understood, the resultant mush was discarded and the head was filled with resin-impregnated linen.

With work on the skull complete, the undertakers turned their attention to the abdomen which had to be cleared of all its organs. Initially this was accomplished by means of a vertical cut made high in the left side, but this was soon replaced by a lower cut, still on the left side but now running from the hip bone to the pubic region. The knife used was invariably one of obsidian or "Ethiopian stone" as this had ritual significance. All the contents of the abdomen, apart from the kidneys which were not considered important, were removed and stored.

The diaphragm was then cut in order to allow the removal of the lungs and the cleaning of the chest cavity. It was essential that the heart – thought to be the centre of intellect and emotion – was left inside the body; hearts which removed by accident were quickly stitched back into place.

As the skin would shrink during drying, the carefully trimmed fingernails and toenails were secured with twine. The empty body was then washed and packed with temporary stuffing material before being placed on a sloping board where it was covered with powdered natron.

 # DESICCATION

At first sight it seems curious that Egypt's embalmers chose to use an artificial drying agent. However, although the Red Land offered a readily available and natural means of dehydrating the body, it would have proved very difficult to control the temporary interment and subsequent exhumation of hundreds of corpses in the desert sands. Furthermore, prolonged burial in hot sand left the body's skin tanned, leathery and unnaturally rigid.

While sand was always available for use in an emergency – a group of soldiers who fell in battle during the 11th Dynasty was returned home for burial still coated in the sand which had dried their bodies – it was not regarded as suitable for every day use. Nor was it practical to consider drying large numbers of bodies by the natural heat of the sun or a hot fire.

The drying properties of salt, used for centuries to preserve fish, were well known but ignored. Instead the undertakers turned to natron, a naturally occurring drying agent with mild antiseptic properties which had been used as a ritual purifier for many years. Natron, a crystalline mixture of sodium carbonate and sodium bicar-

ABOVE: ALEXANDER THE
GREAT DEPICTED IN A
MOSAIC FROM POMPEII.

convey the essence of the process to his readers. This was misunderstood by early Egyptologists, who assumed that the natron must have been used in a concentrated solution form, with the corpses reclining in giant baths or bobbing upright in huge watertight pickling vats. The practical difficulties involved in soaking the bodies would have been extraordinary, and it follows that no trace of any form of giant embalming vessel has ever been recovered from any archaeological site.

Recent research involving the preservation of rats and birds has shown that natron solution does little to enhance preservation; human bodies treated in this way would be in danger of disintegrating into an unpleasant sludge, while those that did survive being bathed in natron would consequently be liable to shed their softened skin. This would make them extremely difficult to stuff and bandage.

Modern experimentation has proved what common sense would suggest; the most effective and simplest method of using the natron would have been to heap it dry in and around the body.

Tradition holds that there was one other preserving agent used in Egypt. Alexander the Great, who died of fever in 323 BC, was reportedly embalmed in a glass coffin filled with honey. However, as Alexander died in Babylon, we may assume that he was embalmed before the long journey back to Alexandria. The method would therefore appear to be a Babylonian one. The efficacy of the method – and the truth of the story – are not yet proven.

bonate containing traces of sodium chloride and sodium sulphate, could be collected from the shores of the lakes in the Wadi en-Natrun, which lay some 72 km (45 miles) from Memphis in the desert to the west of the Nile Delta.

Herodotus, writing in Greek, correctly tells us that the natron was heaped around the eviscerated body. However, he was handicapped by a lack of appropriate words. The Greeks did not embalm their dead and, without a precise translation for "mummification", he was forced to use a word whose literal meaning "to salt-dry fish" would

STORAGE OF THE ENTRAILS

RIGHT: WOODEN FIGURES
OF PTAH-SOKER-OSIRIS
SOMETIMES HID PAPYRUS
SCROLLS INSCRIBED
WITH EXCERPTS FROM
THE BOOK OF THE DEAD.

As the body slowly dried on its bier, the embalmers turned their attention to the entrails. The organs removed from the chest and abdomen were in turn washed, dried, anointed, coated in hot resin and wrapped in the finest linen. The plain storage jars used to house the viscera during the Old Kingdom had evolved into ornate stone or pottery vessels

whose human-headed stoppers were intended to represent the deceased. Today these jars are known as canopic jars, the name being derived from the Greek story of Canopus, pilot of King Menelaus, who was worshipped in the Nile Delta in the form of a vessel with a bloated body and a human head.

During the 19th Dynasty the human-headed

stoppers were replaced by stoppers representing the heads of the four sons of the god Horus: Imset, the human-headed son who guarded the liver and who was in turn protected by the goddess Isis; Hapy, baboon-headed protector of the lungs who was linked with the goddess Nephthys; Qebhsenuef, falcon-headed guardian of the intestines protected by the goddess Selkis; Duamutef, protector of the stomach guarded by the goddess Neith. By the 21st Dynasty this tradition had been dropped, and the wrapped viscera were replaced in the emptied abdomen before bandaging; by the 26th Dynasty the packages were simply placed between the legs. Empty or even solid "dummy" Canopic jars were still included in the funerary equipment, but these now had a purely symbolic meaning.

 # STUFFING THE BODY

ABOVE: THE FOUR CANOPIC JARS, HOUSING THE ENTRAILS OF THE DECEASED.

Some forty days later the drying was deemed complete and the body, now much lighter in weight and much darker in colour, was transferred to the *Wabet*, or House of Purification. Here it was emptied of its temporary stuffing – all of which was saved – and thoroughly washed and dried. The

abdomen was then ready for packing with resin-soaked linen, bags of sawdust or natron crystals, or even dried lichen. Before the abdominal slit was closed the body was massaged with aromatic oils in an attempt to restore a lifelike feel to the stiffened skin. The abdomen could then be pulled or loosely stitched together, the wound magically healed by a gold eye of Horus glued in place by molten resin.

The arms and legs of the now supple corpse had an unnatural, emaciated appearance which contrasted unpleasantly with the rounded stuffed abdomen. The face was frighteningly shrunken and aged. No one wanted to go to the Afterlife in this state and so, from the 21st Dynasty onwards, packing was routinely used to define the features of the face and restore the natural rounded appearance of the limbs. This packing, which could be linen, sawdust, fat, sand or even mud, was introduced through a series of cuts so that it lay between the skin and the underlying tissue. The mummy of Amenhotep III was used as an undertaker's guinea pig: the resin that was stuffed under his skin set as hard as a rock, giving the unfortunate king a most unnatural appearance.

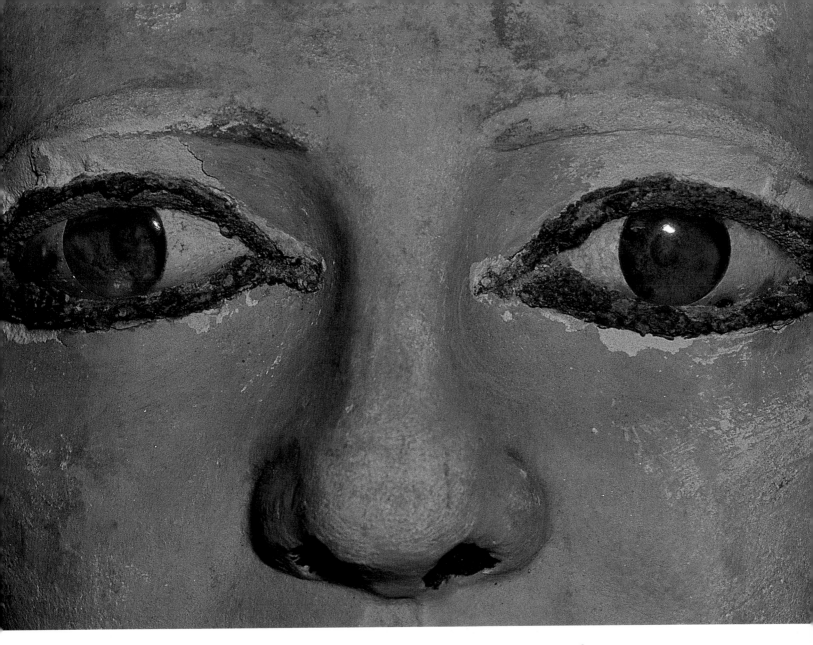

In most cases the tops of the legs could be stuffed via the original embalming cut, but additional cuts might be needed in the knee, ankle, heel, or even between the toes in order to round out the lower leg and foot. The arms and back were packed through a cut in the shoulder, while the cheeks could be rounded via the mouth. The cuts were then sewn together, or glued with resin. It was important not to overstuff the corpse as any subsequent shrinkage might cause the skin to burst. The cheeks of the once-beautiful Princess Henttawi did split in this way; she has recently been restored, by means of invisible stitches and the removal of padding, and is currently displayed in Cairo Museum.

As it was vital that the entire body be preserved, any missing or damaged body parts were restored or replaced at this stage. Modern scientific analysis reveals that it was not uncommon for dynastic mummies to have false legs, hair extensions, artificial eyebrows and even false penises and nipples. One old lady even had her bed sores repaired with leather patches sewn on to her skin. Nothing could be done to save the original eyeballs and so these were pushed down into the socket. Artificial eyes – often semi-precious stones, linen balls or even small onions – helped the dead to see again, while onions were occasionally used to plug the ears or the body cavities. The nostrils were blocked with wax or linen, while the tongue was covered by a sliver of gold. The mummy might then be painted – red for men, yellow for women – with henna applied to the feet and palms, and make-up used to enhance any remaining beauty. Finally, the entire body was covered in molten resin intended to seal and protect it against moisture.

ABOVE: INLAID EYES OF ROCK CRYSTAL AND OPAQUE WHITE QUARTZ APPEAR STRIKINGLY REALISTIC.

LEFT: THE EYE OF HORUS; A POWERFUL AND PROTECTIVE AMULET FOR BOTH THE LIVING AND THE DEAD.

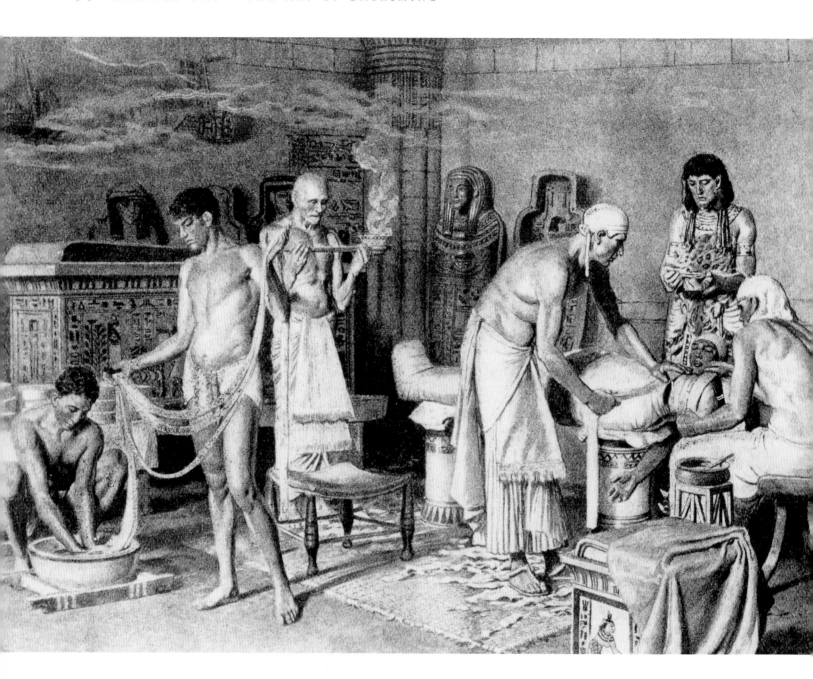

 THE ART OF BANDAGING

ABOVE: AN IMAGINATIVE
19TH-CENTURY
INTERPRETATION OF AN
EMBALMING WORKSHOP.

The wrapping of the mummy was the final stage in the embalming process. This was a laborious task that took 10 to 15 days and required a great deal of expensive cloth. It could not be hurried; tight, even bandages not only enhanced the appearance of the deceased, they literally held the body together, providing a much-needed stiffening and preventing unsightly bulges. The more influential members of society might be fortunate enough to be bandaged in the discarded clothing of sacred statues. This cloth, which had been worn by the statues of the gods, had an enviable aura of sanctity and was in great demand. Others purchased linen from textile shops, while the less wealthy recycled a jumble of old sheets, worn-out clothing, towels and anything else that could be

LEFT: THE HEART SCARAB; ONE OF THE MOST IMPORTANT AMULETS PLACED IN THE MUMMY WRAPPINGS.

BELOW: THIS MUMMY OF A LATE NEW KINGDOM PRIESTESS LIES NEATLY WRAPPED WITHIN ITS ELABORATELY PAINTED COFFIN.

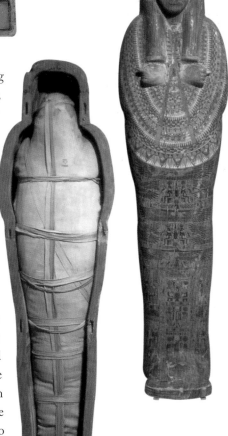

torn into strips and used. One individual was even mummified in an old sail complete with rigging loops.

It has been estimated that in order to bandage a loved-one the family of the deceased would have to provide the undertaker with over 375 square metres (448 square yards) of linen. This linen was graded by the undertakers; the finest cloth was torn into long strips some 6–20 cm (3–8 in) wide, while the remainder was reserved for use as padding. Fortunately, the family would have forty days during the drying period to collect the cloth together. Occasionally, towards the end of the dynastic age, the bandages were dyed red, yellow or blue.

The corpse, lying on its back on a wooden trestle, was first wrapped in a yellow shroud. Then the bandaging started with the individual wrapping of each toe and finger; some mummies had golden finger- and toe-stalls fitted over the bandages at this stage. After wrapping the hands and feet, the undertakers wound a bandage in a figure of eight pattern around the head before wrapping the arms and bandaging them straight along the torso; only royal mummies regularly had their arms crossed over the chest in classic horror-film tradition. Men often had their hands coyly shielding the genitals, while women were wrapped with their hands extended along the thigh. The bandagers then worked down the body from the head to the feet.

As each body part was wrapped spells were spoken for the welfare of the deceased and precious jewellery and protective amulets were incorporated within the layers. The bandages were artfully padded and moulded to ensure that the shape of the mummy – in particular the genitals and the face – was retained;

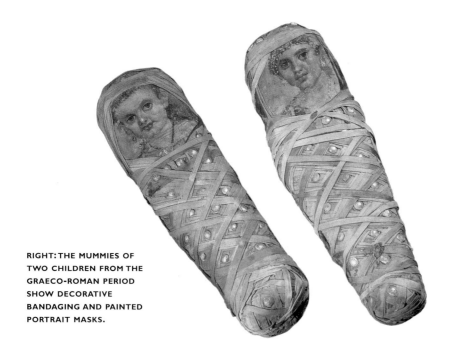

RIGHT: THE MUMMIES OF TWO CHILDREN FROM THE GRAECO-ROMAN PERIOD SHOW DECORATIVE BANDAGING AND PAINTED PORTRAIT MASKS.

any missing limbs were neatly restored with linen rolls. Frequent applications of hot resin effectively glued the bandages in place. Finally, the mummy was dressed in one or more red shrouds knotted at the head and the feet and held in place by wide bandages passing across the body.

During the 21st and 22nd dynasties, well-dressed mummies often wore red leather straps crossed over the top of their bandages. The purpose of these straps is unknown, as is the purpose of the beaded net shrouds which came into vogue during the 25th Dynasty, and which remained popular until the Roman Period. These net shrouds were an expensive indulgence; those who could not afford the real thing made do with a real net, or with a net painted on to the mummy wrappings.

 # THE FINAL TOUCHES

Finally, the mummy mask, an idealized likeness of the deceased encompassing a long wig and a decorated collar, was fitted over the shrouded bundle. It was hoped that this mask, which could in an emergency function as a substitute head, would help the Ka and the Ba to identify their host body within the tomb. Royal masks, like the world famous mask of Tutankhamen, were made of solid gold and inlaid with semi-precious stones. Less wealthy individuals had to make do with masks of moulded cartonnage – a form of papier mâché made from linen stiffened with plaster or resin – which could be painted and gilded to resemble gold. Thus packaged and masked, the body was returned to the family for burial.

The entire process, from death to mummy, had taken seventy days. Herodotus was confused in his belief that the drying period alone lasted seventy days, and indeed modern experimentation has shown that there is no benefit to be gained from drying a corpse for longer than forty days. Seventy days was a mystical period; the length of the eclipse of Sothis, or Sirius the Dog Star, thus linking the death and rebirth of the body with the death and

OPPOSITE: THE GOLDEN MUMMY MASK OF YUYA, FATHER-IN-LAW OF KING AMENHOTEP III.

rebirth of the star. This was the time recorded in Genesis for the mummification and mourning of Jacob: "And forty days were fulfilled for him, for so are fulfilled the days of those which are embalmed; and the Egyptians mourned for him for three score and ten days".

One Old Kingdom mummy seems to have spent an inexplicably long time with the embalmers. Queen Meresankh III was apparently delivered to the House of Mummification in "Year 1, first month of the third season, day 21" and remained there until in "Year 2, second month of the second season, day 18, she went to her beautiful tomb"; a full 272 days before burial. It may be that, as Meresankh was mummified at the very dawn of the science, her embalmers attempted a unique, time-consuming method of desiccation, perhaps even pickling the unfortunate queen in natron solution. However, the wording suggests that she may have been housed, already mummified, in a temporary tomb before her final interment. It may even be that the artisans who recorded these dates on the wall of her Giza tomb made a simple error.

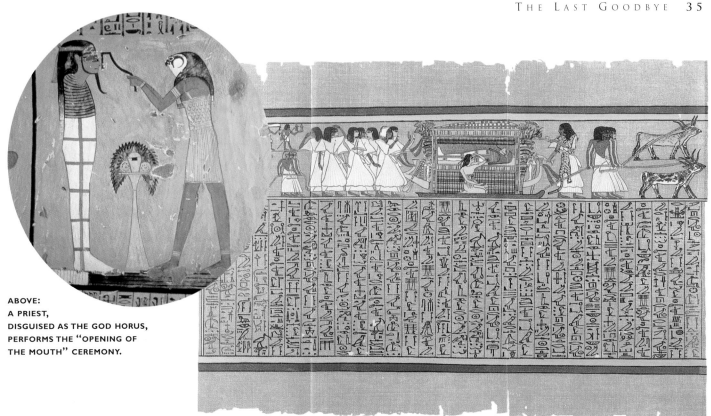

ABOVE:
A PRIEST,
DISGUISED AS THE GOD HORUS,
PERFORMS THE "OPENING OF
THE MOUTH" CEREMONY.

THE LAST GOODBYE

ABOVE: THE COFFIN OF
THE DECEASED IS DRAGGED
ON A SLEDGE TOWARDS
THE TOMB.

The neatly wrapped, sweet-smelling, masked mummy was placed in its mummiform wooden coffin to await burial. While specific funerary practices varied at different times and in different parts of the country, the basic Egyptian funeral ritual remained constant. The mummy was carried to his or her new home, magic was used to ensure that he or she would be reborn, and then the tomb was sealed. Although the majority of Egyptians had a simple ceremony followed by interment in the local cemetery, wealthy families paid for the most elaborate ritual that they could afford; an expensive funeral provided a fitting tribute for the dear departed while conferring great prestige on the grieving relatives.

The full funeral, as practised at Thebes, consisted of four distinct stages, each of which had its own particular rites and spells. Included were the mourning on the east bank of the Nile, the crossing of the river, the procession to the cemetery and the arrival at the tomb. Each stage was supervized by one of several priests who played different roles in ceremonies intended to identify the mummy with the dead Osiris. The long cortege consisted of the coffin carried under a star-spangled canopy, a statue of the deceased, priests, friends and family, plus servants carrying funeral goods and offerings, two women representing Isis and Nephthys and groups of professional female mourners. The procession was greeted at the tomb by a group of ceremonial male dancers and a priest reading aloud from a magical scroll.

Here, in the doorway of the tomb, the important Opening of the Mouth service was performed. The officiating priest donned the jackal-headed mask of Anubis and the mummy was propped upright in its coffin. Two assistant priests touched the mouth of the mummy with a variety of sacred objects, including a ceremonial adze, while spells were recited to ensure that he or she would be able to see, speak, hear, taste and touch in the Afterlife. Effectively, this ritual restored the mummy to life. Afterwards, offerings were made, a funeral banquet was eaten, and the mummy was sealed in the tomb.

OPPOSITE: A LATE PERIOD
FUNERAL STELA SHOWING
THE DECEASED, DRESSED
IN WHITE, STANDING
BEFORE THE GODS OF
THE AFTERLIFE.

LIFE BEYOND DEATH

BELOW: A PRIEST WEARING THE DISTINCTIVE JACKAL MASK OF THE GOD ANUBIS ATTENDS TO THE MUMMY.

The ceremony of the Opening of the Mouth was merely the last in a series of rituals performed over the body since death. The preparation of the dead for burial in modern societies is generally regarded as a secular task even if it leads to a religious ceremony. In Egypt the ritual aspect of the preparation was of overwhelming importance; it was the need to perform the correct rites which ensured that the process took a full seventy days. Even an action as simple as washing the corpse was fraught with ritual undertones.

Mummification was itself considered to be a religious rite and the embalmers – occasionally dressed in ritual masks – took the role of gods performing a sacred ceremony. Some of the rituals seem bizarre to modern eyes: Diodorus Siculus tells us that the graphically named "Ripper" who made the incision in the flank was forced to run away from the embalming table and the curses and stones hurled by his fellow morticians. Each stage of mummification had its own particular spells and rituals; the treatment of the skull, for example, was accompanied by an ancient spell designed to ensure that the deceased might never again lose his head.

WASTE MATTER

As embalming progressed, all the refuse – the used packing, soiled natron, sawdust and cloth – was stored in large pots until it could be returned to the grieving family. This unhygienic stinking debris could not be thrown away as it might contain fragments of the deceased – in particular the bits, such as fingernails that occasionally fell off during drying – which would be needed in the Afterlife. It was essential that this refuse had a proper disposal so that not even the smallest body part fell into enemy hands, and yet there was a reluctance to bury the debris within the tomb as it was considered to be ritually impure. Thus, the tradition of interring the embalming refuse separately, close to the tomb of the deceased, was developed. This could be an onerous task; the embalmer's cache of an 11th Dynasty man named Ipy included seventy-six heavy jars of fluids and powdered matter.

The embalming cache of the boy king Tutankhamen was discovered in 1907, some fifteen years before the secret of his tomb was revealed. The cache had been hidden in a shallow pit not far from the final resting place of the king. Here were found a series of large storage jars holding embalmers' refuse, seal impressions bearing the name of the king, a miniature golden mask, floral collars and the remains of a meal of fowl, mutton, meat and wine. With the subsequent discovery and meticulous recording of the king's tomb it became clear that this cache had originally been abandoned in the then empty entrance corridor. It had been moved from the tomb after an attempted robbery, when the decision was taken to block the corridor with rubble.

LOOK WHO'S COMING TO DINNER

The end of the 22nd Dynasty heralded a slow and steady decline in standards of mummification, with attention now focused on the increasingly intricate bandaging rather than on the preservation of the corpse within. The Late Period saw the introduction of the black, bitumen-like resin as a consolidating agent; this, poured through the embalming incision, soaked through to the very bones, darkening the appearance and making the mummies surprisingly heavy. Mummification was now no longer the preserve of the rich, or indeed of the Egyptians. The foreigners who had settled in Egypt had adopted local customs, and they too wanted to be mummified before burial. As more and more undertakers processed larger numbers of bodies, methods grew increasingly slipshod.

Those who paid for the service could not see beneath the artfully arranged wrappings and were no doubt delighted by the diamond patterning, gold studs and gilded masks which now adorned their dear departed. Modern X-ray analysis has confirmed, however, that many of these later mummies, outwardly perfect, contain a jumble of disarticulated and unrelated bones plus pottery, mud, wood, and other extraneous matter. Conditions in the mortuary were chaotic, and it was not unusual for the remains of two or more individuals to be mixed together. Some unscrupulous undertakers shortened the bodies by breaking the bones and discarding unwanted pieces, presumably so that they could sell the relatives an unsuitably short coffin.

The cartonnage mummy masks were by now mass-produced, with no pretence at accurate or individual portraiture. Badly modelled and often most un-lifelike, the defects in their workmanship were concealed beneath showy layers of golden paint. Some of these masks were even made from scrap papyrus rather than linen; archaeologists are now able to extract and read some of the texts accidentally preserved in this way.

Mummies had become as much objects of art as religious symbols. Several classical authors, including Herodotus, Diodorus Siculus and Cicero, mention the Egyptian habit – unsavoury to the fastidious Greeks and Romans who were accustomed to cremating their dead – of putting their late relatives on public display. There seems little question that mummies were stored, propped upright, in a domestic context, although it is possible that they were kept in a purpose-built shrine or cupboard rather than in the family living room. The bodies were not accorded undue respect. Many of the Graeco-Roman mummies recovered by Flinders Petrie from Hawara show signs of wear and tear; they are dirty, chipped and, in at least one case, covered in childish graffiti.

Private Egyptians had always venerated their dead relations; now it seems that the ancestor cults were taking their extreme logical form. The body of the revered ancestor made a convenient focus for devotions. Once the family had lost interest in their family mummy – perhaps because all immediate descendants had died – it was accorded a brief, cursory funeral, often ending up in an unmarked grave. Herodotus believed that the mummy or its effigy was intended to serve as a permanent reminder of man's mortality:

> *At upper class social gatherings, when the banquet is ended, a servant carries round to the guests a coffin in which there is the wooden image of a corpse, carved in as life-like a manner as possible … As he shows it to each guest in turn the servant says "'Gaze upon this, drink and be merry. For when you die, you too will be reduced to this"*

It seems unlikely that this interpretation is true. To the Egyptians the mummy represented life, not death.

BELOW: THE GREEK HISTORIAN HERODOTUS; THE FIRST PERSON TO DESCRIBE THE PROCESS OF MUMMIFICATION.

MASKS AND PORTRAITS

Garishly painted Greek-style plaster masks with lifelike inlaid eyes were fashionable in the Roman Period cemeteries of Middle Egypt. These masks,

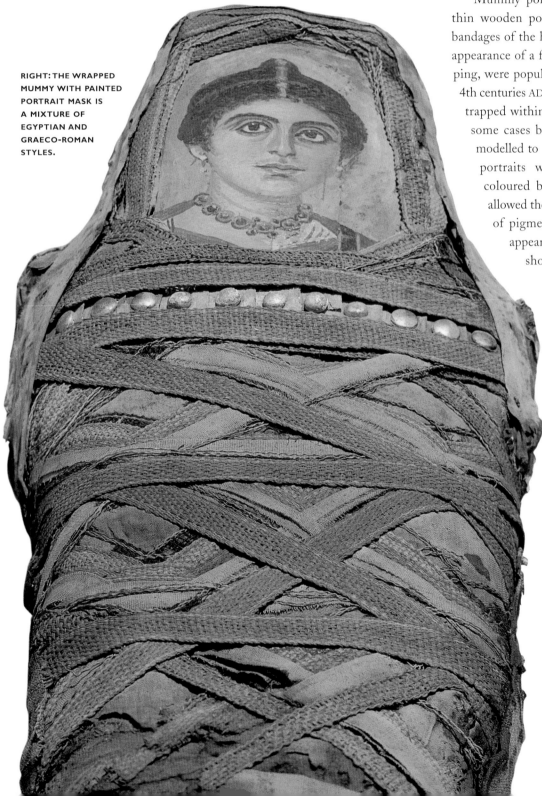

RIGHT: THE WRAPPED MUMMY WITH PAINTED PORTRAIT MASK IS A MIXTURE OF EGYPTIAN AND GRAECO-ROMAN STYLES.

originally fitting flat against the face, were soon placed on the mummy at an angle, to give the impression that the head was resting on a pillow.

Mummy portraits, or "Faiyumic portraits", thin wooden portrait boards inserted into the bandages of the head so as to give the unnerving appearance of a face peeping out from the wrapping, were popular in Egypt from the 1st to the 4th centuries AD. This impression of a living body trapped within the bandages was enhanced in some cases by the use of realistic footcases, modelled to show sandalled or bare feet. The portraits were painted in encaustic, or coloured beeswax, a new medium which allowed the artist to build up multiple layers of pigment, giving a hauntingly lifelike appearance. The intention was now to show the dead person as an individual, rather than as a standardized form of Osiris. The realism of the best examples suggest that the portraits were commissioned from specialized artists during the deceased's lifetime.

The high turnover of bodies in the embalmer's workshop meant that there was a very real danger of mixing up the mummies. One wrapped body looked very much like another, and so in order to avoid embarrassment a system of tagging was introduced. Each mummy was provided with a wooden identity label which recorded details of name, age, and occasionally parentage and date of death. These labels, written in black ink in Greek and/or Egyptian, were tied around the neck and

proved a permanent means of identification for those bodies which were to be interred without a coffin in a communal tomb, and were useful when a mummy had to be transported from the place of death to the family burial ground. One Greek lady, Senpamouthes, posted her mother's body to her brother with the casual instruction that he would recognize his mummy by both her attached label as well as her pink shroud which had her name written on the abdomen.

 # THE END OF AN ERA

The tradition of mummification had lasted for over thirty centuries, stretching from the middle of the Old Kingdom to the end of the Graeco-Roman period. However, the 1st Century AD saw the arrival of Christianity in Egypt. By the 4th Century Christianity was challenging the ancient pagan religion. The Christians, or Copts, believed that they would cast off their earthly body on death and therefore chose a simple burial; intact, unembalmed and without grave goods. Dressed in simple tunics, or wrapped in a sheet, the Coptic bodies lay flat on their backs to await their god. It is perhaps Egyptology's greatest irony that the Copts, who cared so little for the preservation of the corpse, were allowed to lie undisturbed in their tombs.

The old religion coexisted for a time alongside the new, but as Christianity spread through Egypt, mummification quietly died away.

the FATE *of the* PHARAOHS

Egypt's changing social structure, and her evolving religious beliefs, are reflected in her architecture of death.

A TOMB WITH A VIEW

Throughout the Old Kingdom the pharaoh was all powerful; a living demi-god who, solely among all the Egyptians, could communicate with the great deities who controlled Egypt's destiny. In death, too, the king was the only Egyptian who could hope for an Afterlife away from the tomb. Surrounding the pharaoh was a small, intimate group of courtiers, most of whom were linked to their monarch by marriage. These courtiers fully expected to continue their association with the king beyond the grave and into the afterlife, therefore, the pharaoh built their tombs around his own great pyramid.

The Middle Kingdom saw a gradual diffusion of authority away from the court. The king still wielded immense power, but a new decentralization meant that there was a greater emphasis on local government. Provincial dignitaries, at last eligible to enter the Field of Reeds, had no further need to associate themselves with the dead king. Instead, they built their own tombs in local cemeteries, making use of local materials and taking account of local conditions. The old desert cemeteries remained suited to the construction of masonry-built tombs while the geography of Middle and Upper Egypt encouraged the development of rock-cut tombs situated high in the cliffs which bordered the Nile.

By the time of the New Kingdom, Egypt's ever-increasing wealth had led to an insatiable demand for scribes, accountants and architects. This was the age of the middle classes, who were now richer than ever before. They too could look forward to an Afterlife with Osiris, and so chose to invest their new-found wealth in making provision for death. Each local cemetery was now home to a great variety of tombs, ranging in style from the simple to the magnificent.

The foreigners who settled in Egypt at the end of the dynastic age adapted to these local traditions while retaining some of their own customs. While the ordinary Egyptians continued as they had done for centuries, the Egyptian elite now absorbed Greek influences into their burial traditions and the Greek settlers reciprocated by incorporating Egyptian traditions into theirs. The result was a hybrid Graeco-Egyptian style of provincial tomb.

OPPOSITE: THE DECEASED SENNEDJEM AND HIS WIFE RECEIVE OFFERINGS FROM HIS KA PRIEST.

PROVIDING FOR DEATH

The grave provided a permanent home for the Ka, or spirit, after death. This idea of a house or home was taken very literally. Under ideal circumstances the Ka would appreciate the same facilities that the deceased had enjoyed in life; spacious living quarters including a private chamber to house the body and its entrails, plus a reception area to allow communication with visitors. The most elaborate of Egypt's early tombs even included a lavatory for the Ka, while some later tombs were set in beautiful gardens. The simple pit graves, still used by the poor, were clearly no longer suitable for the upper classes.

The early private tombs were stuffed with a vast array of goods, all of which were deemed necessary for use in the Afterlife. The richer the individual in life, the more grave goods he or she would require in death. Stone and pottery vessels, furniture, tools and weapons, clothing, cosmetics, jewellery, musical instruments, toys and board games were all provided. Perversely, the king, who was richest of all, had less need of grave goods than most. He could rely on the loyalty of his priests who would, for all time, bring daily offerings to nourish the royal Ka.

It was vital that the Ka had access to food and drink, and so beef, bread and wine were routinely provided in the tomb. Occasionally this food was set out in the form of an eternal banquet; the best-preserved example of this is the 2nd Dynasty tomb of an elderly woman buried at Sakkara which included a full dinner laid out on the floor. The menu included a loaf of bread, barley porridge, roast fish, pigeon stew, roast quail, cooked kidneys, ribs of beef, stewed figs, fresh berries, honey cakes and cheese, all to be washed down with wine. In life the lady tomb owner would have been unable to eat such a chewy meal as she had a deformed jaw. In death, her disability would have been magically cured.

Soon it was realized that, no matter how many grave goods were provided, it would never be possible to supply enough food to nourish the Ka for all eternity. Nor was it possible to rely on the immediate family to continue bringing offerings to the tomb; the deceased probably knew all too well how easy it was to overlook these tiresome

familial obligations. A back-up system had to be put into place.

The establishment of Ka priests (priests dedicated to the service of the cult of the deceased) was an obvious step. To pay for this service, the prudent tomb owner would endow his tomb with a bequest of agricultural land. The produce from this land provided both offerings for the Ka and payment for the priest and his descendants. The only fly in this ointment was that legal title to the land may be lost at times of economic and political instability. If the funds disappeared, the service would stop.

Magic offered a better and certainly more permanent solution. Symbolic or substitute grave goods could be provided in the form of small models, or painted or engraved images which, in the Afterlife, would magically come to life in order to represent a real person or item. A tomb owner whose walls were decorated with images of food and drink could therefore rest in peace, assured of a perpetual banquet.

From this time onwards tombs were designed with relatively little storage space, but with a great expanse of wall to hold the magical scenes. At first the scenes were concerned with the material goods which would be required by the deceased within the tomb. Later, as the prospect of entering the Field of Reeds was opened to all, the scenes included images of the deceased and his family enjoying life with Osiris.

ABOVE: EGYPT'S NOBLE-WOMEN ENJOY THE DELIGHTS OF A BANQUET.

OPPOSITE: THE DECEASED IS TRANSFIGURED BY THE DIVINE WATER OF LIFE.

A WASTEFUL PRACTICE

ABOVE: A WOODEN MODEL
OF A BREWERY PROVIDED TO
PRODUCE MAGICAL BEER
FOR THE DECEASED.

RIGHT: SHABTI FIGURES
WOULD SERVE THEIR
MASTER FOR ALL ETERNITY.

FAR RIGHT: MINIATURE
GOLD COFFINS, SUCH
AS THIS ONE, HOUSED
THE ENTRAILS OF
TUTANKHAMEN.

A dead pharaoh could not be expected to attend to his own needs. He would certainly need servants to assist him for all eternity. The archaic kings of Egypt took a very practical approach to this servant problem. Their own regal tombs were surrounded by subsidiary graves, designed to house not only the high-ranking courtiers whom we might expect to find in a royal cemetery, but also the members of the king's personal entourage – the royal servants, dwarfs, ladies of the harem and even pet dogs. We have no evidence to indicate how these attendants met their end, but it is possible that they were either killed or forced to commit suicide following the death of the king.

Such practices are known from other ancient Near Eastern societies. In 2650 BC the divine kings and queens of Ur were accompanied in death by their female attendants. A mass grave, now known as the Great Death Pit, has yielded the remains of six men and sixty-eight women. These women appear to have gone to their deaths willingly, taking poison in order to ensure that they would continue to serve their royal masters in the next world.

With the development of the idea of symbolic magic this wasteful practice could be abandoned. Now it was possible for the upper classes to include a miniature model servant in the tomb who would, in the Afterlife, come to life and work for his or her master. These wooden or stone figures, painted and plastered in a most lifelike fashion, were depicted in the act of performing routine duties, such as baking bread or brewing beer – tasks which they would be happy to perform for all eternity.

This concept was later extended to the provision of *shabti* figures – small funerary figurines of wood, stone or metal in the shape of a bandaged mummy. A powerful spell engraved on each figure ensured that it would function correctly: the first duty of any shabti, when called upon by its master, was to reply "here I am". To help them with their work, many shabtis carried agricultural implements – hoes, mattocks or baskets – in their bandaged arms. Tombs which were endowed with a large number of shabtis would also include a slightly larger foreman figure to oversee the work gangs. These foremen shabtis could be distinguished by their larger size, their everyday clothes and their whips.

WONDERFUL THINGS

Although there was now no need to include a multitude of everyday goods within the tomb, private individuals were still buried with a few treasured personal items. The undertakers hid these and valuable jewellery and amulets within their bandages. Jewellery specifically designed to be worn by mummies is usually quite distinctive; it was generally made of fragile wafer-thin metal and often lacked the fasteners of everyday jewellery. Draped across an immobile body, however, this false fiery functioned as the real thing.

The jewellery was not simply used to decorate the corpse, it also offered the hope of magical protection to the deceased. The amulets had an even more specific purpose. Their form, location and function were decreed by long tradition, although some undertakers seem to have been less certain than others where the various charms should be sited. The heart – home of the intellect and emotion – was of vital importance to the deceased and needed special protection. It was crucial that the mummy be provided with Chapter 30B of *The Book of the Dead* engraved on a stylized heart of green stone mounted in gold and worn at the throat. This amulet would prevent the heart from betraying the Ka before the tribunal of the gods: "Do not act against me as a hostile witness. Do not oppose me before the tribunal. Do not tilt the scales against me …"

Kings, adhering to the old traditions, were provided with a combination of ritual goods – items such as shabtis which would be useful in the next life – plus consumer goods intended for the use of the Ka within the tomb. The tomb of Tutankhamen, by no means lavish by royal standards, yielded in Howard Carter's often quoted words "strange animals, statues, and gold – everywhere the glint of gold". Included in the tomb were furniture, clothing, shoes, perfumes and cosmetics, chariots, weapons, food and wine and much, much more. So many precious items had been crammed into the limited space that it was to take ten years for Carter to record the tomb and empty it of its contents.

Tutankhamen's mummy, adorned with a golden face mask and golden hands, lay inside three coffins. The outer two were made of wood, coated in plaster and covered in gold embellished with inlays of semi-precious stones. The innermost coffin was solid gold; it has been estimated to be worth at least one million pounds (1,700,000 US dollars) scrap value. The true monetary value of such a piece would, of course, be beyond price. Within his mummy wrappings were hidden some 150 jewels and amulets. Surrounding the massive stone sarcophagus were three wooden shrines, again decorated in gold. Even the king's entrails were stored in a golden canopic shrine. All this splendour was provided for the burial of a short-lived, relatively insignificant monarch. We can only

RIGHT: THE PAPER-
THIN SANDALS OF
TUTANKHAMEN, DESIGNED
FOR WEAR IN THE
AFTERLIFE.

FAR RIGHT: THE GOLD MASK
OF KING TUTANKHAMEN.

BELOW: UPPER-CLASS
EGYPTIAN TOMBS
CONTAINED EVERYTHING
THAT MIGHT BE REQUIRED
IN THE AFTERLIFE,
INCLUDING SUITES OF
FURNITURE. THE CHAIR
BELONGING TO THE
PRINCESS SITAMEN WAS
FOUND IN THE TOMB OF
HER GRANDPARENTS.

begin to guess at the magnificence of the equipment which must have been provided for Egypt's greatest kings.

When Howard Carter lifted the lid of Tutankhamen's innermost coffin he saw an amazing sight:

Before us, occupying the whole interior of the golden coffin, was an impressive, neat and carefully made mummy, over which had been poured anointing unguents … in great quantity – consolidated and blackened by age. In contradiction to the general dark and sombre effect, due to these unguents, was a brilliant, one might say magnificent, burnished gold mask or similitude of the king, covering his head and shoulders, which, like the feet, had been intentionally avoided when using the unguents.

Some thirty centuries ago the priests who conducted the royal funeral ceremony anointed their dead king with unguents and perfumes as part of the time-honoured purification ritual. Unfortunately these resin-based fluids had the effect of glue, sticking both the king and his mask to the coffin. The mummy could not be removed from the coffin, therefore, if the body was to be examined, it would have to be unwrapped within the tomb. The same unguents had penetrated deep into the bandages, causing a form of slow spontaneous combustion and reducing the fine linen to sooty powder. This made it extremely difficult to determine the order of wrapping although it was apparent that the toes, fingers and limbs had been individually wrapped, that linen had been used to pad the body, and that the penis had been wrapped in an erect position.

Once the remains of the bandages had been cleared away it was possible to see the abdominal embalming cut situated on the left side of the body close to the navel. The king's spindly legs and folded arms were revealed, as was his pallid and poorly preserved skin. However, it was still not possible to release the king's head from its gold mask. Howard Carter feared that "it would require a hammer and chisel to free it" but happily he succeeded with the aid of hot knives. Underneath the mask Tutankhamen's face was tolerably well preserved but covered in brittle, cracked skin, marred by white spots caused by natron damage. The scientists could see that the king's head was shaven, his ears were pierced and his lips had been glued shut with resin. Later it became apparent that his brain was missing. Although the nostrils and eye sockets had been plugged before wrapping, the nose had been flattened beneath the bandages.

Professor Douglas Derry, the anatomist who conducted this preliminary autopsy, deduced that the king had died a young man approximately 18 years of age and standing some 1.7 metres (5 ft 5 in) tall. It was generally assumed that the king had died of tuberculosis although there was no evidence to support this diagnosis. In 1968, an X-ray analysis of the body was able to suggest a more plausible cause of death; a small piece of bone lodged within the skull cavity indicated that Tutankhamen had suffered a fatal head injury. Whether this was an accident or murder it is not possible to say.

The young king's viscera were housed in golden canopic jars shaped like miniature mummi-form coffins and stored in a beautiful white stone canopic chest. Two further miniature coffins were found in a plain wooden box casually stacked in the treasury. These coffins, both of which had been coated in thick black resin, each yielded a smaller golden coffin holding a mummified fetus. The first mummy, a premature baby girl some 30 cm (1 ft) in length, wore a golden funerary mask. The second baby, also a girl, had died at or soon after birth. An autopsy conducted by Professor Derry showed that she had suffered from Sprengal's deformity, an illness causing spina bifida and scoliosis. No explanation was provided for the presence of the two babies in the tomb, but it seems safe to assume that they represent the dead daughters of Tutankhamen.

ROBBERY AND DESTRUCTION

ABOVE: ONE OF THE MANY AMULETS WHICH PROVIDED MAGICAL PROTECTION FOR THE BODY OF TUTANKHAMEN.

Unfortunately, almost all of Egypt's wealthy graves were looted in antiquity, some almost as soon as they had been sealed. The ever-present tomb robbers, the scourge of Egypt's cemeteries, ensured that few of the dead were left undisturbed. Their valuables were just too tempting. Those graves which did survive intact were usually those, such as the tomb of Tutankhamen, which were preserved by accident. In the case of Tutankhamen, the entrance to the tomb was hidden beneath tons of rubbish dumped during the subsequent excavation of the tomb of Ramesses VI. Even so, at least two bands of thieves had already managed to rob the king.

The first robbery – or phase of robbery – occurred soon after Tutankhamen was buried and may even have been carried out by members of his burial party. At this time the entrance corridor was empty, save for the jars containing the king's embalming waste plus the remains of the funeral feast. Passing into the antechamber the thieves rifled through the neatly stored goods in a search of specific items; precious metal, linen, oils and cosmetics. Discovery was sudden and swift and, forced to flee, the robbers dropped an assortment of loot in the entrance corridor. Fragments of gold, a bronze arrowhead and a bronze staple were all left behind. The priests who restored the tomb decided to block the access corridor with large quanitities of limestone chips in an attempt to prevent a repetition of the crime. The king's embalming waste was removed and given a separate burial close to the tomb.

The local criminals soon rose to the challenge. By tunnelling through the rubble and cutting through the blocked walls, they were able to gain access to all the chambers in the tomb. Fortunately, although the outer shrine was opened, the thieves never reached the mummy itself. These thieves targeted the jewellery which would have been easy to take back via the narrow tunnel. They were very successful; Howard Carter estimated that they

managed to steal about a sixth of the original jewellery. Once again the thieves were caught in the act and the tomb was restored by the necropolis priests. The holes in the internal walls were blocked and plastered over, the corridor was refilled and the tomb was sealed for eternity.

If it was desirable to protect the grave goods from thieves it was, of course, essential to preserve the mummified body. Destruction of the mummy would, as everyone knew, cause the deceased to die the dreaded Second Death. However, it was common knowledge that all mummy wrappings concealed jewellery and amulets which, being valuable, portable and easy to recycle, were a source of great temptation. As it was the inclusion of these precious items within the tomb which attracted the thieves, the answer was simple. Omit the valuable grave goods, and the mummies would be left in peace. Unfortunately, no one was willing to make this sacrifice because the need for protection offered by their jewellery and amulets was vital.

Successful robbers, having penetrated the tomb, tended to head straight for the mummy. Coffins could provide no defence. Although some models were fitted with ingenious locks designed to hold the lid in place, the thieves simply hacked their way through the wood. Royal coffins, made of metal, provided more of a challenge, but could all eventually be opened. Similarly, a stone sarcophagus, although an inconvenience, proved to be no real deterrent. Once they had reached the burial chamber the robbers had all the time in the world to lever off the heaviest lid, or smash the sarcophagus to pieces. Then, clearly untroubled by thoughts of desecrating corpses or the curse of the mummy's tomb, they hacked the body to bits in a devastating search for valuables. The flesh, bones and bandages were cast aside, or were burned in order to extract all the metal hidden within. The robbers of one Theban tomb even used the burning bodies of mummified children to light the dark burial chamber.

ABOVE: EVEN A HEAVY STONE SARCOPHAGUS COULD OFFER LITTLE PROTECTION AGAINST DETERMINED THIEVES.

SECURITY IN THE CEMETERY

Secrecy was obviously the best form of defence. A hidden mummy soon became a forgotten mummy and therefore a safe mummy. However, secrecy in the royal graveyard was almost impossible to achieve. No one could hide a pyramid, and indeed, no one wanted to try. Pyramids were designed to be seen; they were built as a visible testament to the power of the king. Unfortunately, just as everyone could see a pyramid, so they soon came to realize that it must house valuable goods. Old Kingdom architects experimented with an array of physical barriers – hidden entrances, false chambers, underground storage, stone portcullises and backfilled passages – but all to no avail. Even when the kings of the New Kingdom abandoned the flamboyant pyramid in favour of hidden rock-cut tombs excavated in the remote Theban Valley of the Kings, they could not avoid the necropolis thieves. Ineni, architect of Tuthmosis I, the first king to lie in the valley, boasted that he had built his master's tomb "none seeing, none hearing". Unfortunately, Ineni was wrong.

In many cases, robbers were all too aware of the best route into a tomb. The labourers who built the royal tombs, as well as the security guards and priests who were paid to protect them, were by no means trustworthy. Their local knowledge coupled with their individual skills as stonecutters or tunnellers made them particularly adept criminals, while, as locals, they knew precisely who could be bribed to turn a blind eye. In other cases the crimes were clearly opportunistic. Labourers digging a new shaft might easily stumble across a wealthy burial, and few could resist such temptation.

The necropolis officials were not blind to the problem. They conducted regular tours of inspection, during which they listed the tombs in need of restoration. The official records which recorded the locations of the tombs were a closely guarded secret. From the 19th Dynasty onwards no casual

ABOVE: THE VILLAGE AT DEIR EL-MEDINA; HOME TO THE WORKMEN WHO LABOURED IN THE VALLEY OF THE KINGS.

LEFT: THE SPHINX; SILENT SENTINEL OF THE GIZA PYRAMIDS.

workers were allowed to enter the Valley of the Kings. All the labourers were compelled to live at Deir el-Medina, a purpose-built village. Here strict security measures were in force. The village itself was walled and may well have been roofed. The two gates were guarded, and all goods entering and leaving were examined by guards. Nevertheless, the royal graves remained highly vulnerable.

The public cemeteries were also plagued by thieves. The grave-diggers who interred the deceased were all too often those who returned not long after to strip their graves; in some cases the displaced bodies were still pliable – and therefore very recently buried – when robbed. With their specific knowledge of the contents of the graves, cemetery officials were able to target those with the richest pickings, often tunnelling unobserved from one wealthy burial to another, bypassing the poorer internments. This state of affairs, unnoticed in antiquity, becomes all too apparent when modern archaeologists start to excavate.

Even the undertaker could not be considered above suspicion. Friends and family had no means of knowing what went on below the bandages. Some mummies, with perfect outer wrappings, had clearly lost their valuables before the final shrouds were applied. The most blatant example of undertakers robbing a tomb comes from the burial of the 21st Dynasty Princess Henttawi. She was interred in a tomb whose bolted wooden door allowed later bodies to be added. Her burial was followed by that of Princess Djedmutesankh and then by that of Henttawi the second. During the latter's funeral, her two tomb-companions were attacked, their bandages cut and torn in a hurried search for jewellery. The robbers then concealed their crime by pulling the outer shrouds back over the damage. Finally a fourth body, that of Menkheperre, was added to the tomb; his under-takers went a step further, cutting the gilded faces from the three other coffins and again covering up their crime with strategically placed linen shrouds. Much later this tomb was used as a mummy store-

ABOVE: THE VALLEY OF THE KINGS BEFORE THE ARRIVAL OF TOURISTS.

RIGHT: THE OVERSTUFFED CHEEKS OF PRINCESS HENTTAWI BURST OPEN AS SHE LAY IN HER COFFIN; THEY HAVE SINCE BEEN RESTORED.

room. As more and more coffins were crammed into the limited space, the older coffins were simply thrown out.

Tomb robbing was clearly profitable, but it was hard physical work and could be dangerous. Occasionally the thief himself came to grief. In the Rikka cemetery, shaft 124 led down to a stone-cut burial chamber whose roof had collapsed in antiquity. Modern excavation of this chamber revealed the remains of two flattened skeletons. One, the original occupant of the tomb, lay crushed in his coffin. The other, represented by a pair of arm bones on top of the coffin plus a jumble of bones on the floor, was a thief who had been squashed by a rockfall just as he reached out towards the defenceless mummy. The mummy, intact but badly damaged by the rockfall, later yielded a beautiful set of golden jewellery.

The late 20th Dynasty, a time of weak government, high inflation and food shortages, saw tomb robbery established as a way of life at Thebes. So worrying was the situation and so blatant the thefts, that a team of inspectors was sent to report on the state of affairs in the royal necropolis. The team, led by Paser, the mayor of Eastern Thebes, examined both royal and private tombs from the 11th to 18th Dynasties. They discovered that, while the royal burials were still substantially intact – presumably because they were well guarded – many of the private burials had been desecrated and their contents lost: "… the thieves had robbed them all, dragging their owners from their coffins and abandoning them in the desert and stealing their grave goods plus the gold and silver fittings which decorated their coffins". Who was responsible? All the evidence pointed to Paweraa, mayor of Western Thebes. Paser the good mayor disappeared soon after filing his report, leaving Paweraa free to continue his life of crime.

With bribery and corruption rife, the thieves were rarely brought to justice. When they were caught, however, the miscreants inevitably pleaded that the tomb in question was already open: the ancient equivalent of "it wasn't me, gov." One unlucky gang, the robbers of the tomb of King Sebekemsaf, was forced to make a detailed confession:

We went to rob the tombs, as is our usual habit … We broke into the pyramid of this king … We found the noble mummy of the king … a large number of amulets and golden ornaments were round his neck, and he was wearing a golden crown. The noble mummy of the king was completely covered in gold and his coffins were decorated inside and out with gold and silver, and inlaid with every sort of precious stone. We collected the gold that we found on the mummy of the god together with his amulets and jewels … We found the queen lying in exactly the same state and we took all that we found on her … We set fire to their coffins … We took all the objects of gold, silver and bronze and divided it between us.

ABOVE: A MALE MUMMY RECOVERED FROM THE CACHE IN THE TOMB OF AMENHOTEP II.

Tomb robbery was considered a very serious offence, attacking as it did the very survival of the deceased in the Afterlife. The penalties for those caught stealing or handling the stolen goods were severe. Suspects could expect to be beaten or tortured during interrogation – court documents often mention that "X was examined with the aid of the stick and the birch and the screw" – while those found guilty faced a horrible death by impaling on a stake, or banishment to the dreaded forced-labour gangs who toiled in Egypt's mines. The unfortunate incense-roaster Nesamun, accused of theft, was required to swear an oath: "If I tell a lie may I be mutilated and sent to Ethiopia". At first Nesamun refused to talk, but then "he was examined with the stick again. He said 'stop! I will tell all …'".

SAVING THE PHARAOHS

ABOVE: BOUND PRISONERS DEPICTED ON THE WALL OF THE TOMB OF KING SETI I IN THE VALLEY OF THE KINGS.

RIGHT: THE LADY RAY: AN EXCELLENT EXAMPLE OF 18TH DYNASTY MUMMIFICATION.

FAR RIGHT: THE MUMMY OF PINODJEM I; THE KING'S BODY HAS SINCE BEEN LOST.

jewels and amulets. The impoverished government laid claim to all goods salvaged in this way, together with all valuables recovered from the tombs. Indeed, it seems likely that many of the "restored" mummies had been intact before they came to the notice of the government officials. The priests who guarded the necropolis now spent a great deal of time searching for tombs to rob. This brutal despoiling could perhaps be justified on the grounds of protecting the mummies from future thefts. However, it would be naive to accept the restoration as a simple act of piety. Tomb robbery had by now grown into a

By the 21st Dynasty security within the royal necropolis had completely broken down. The royal burials were now in a disgraceful condition. Many of the tombs had been looted, their doorways left open to all, and the royal mummies, stripped of their valuables and often of their bandages, were simply lying where they had been dropped by the callous thieves. The Theban priests of Amen, who were concerned about the security of their own predecessors, decided upon a rescue mission.

Clearly the priests could not attempt to restore each individual burial to its former glory. The time and expense involved would be considerable and, even if such a restoration could be achieved, it would then be impossible to guarantee the security of the refurbished tombs. However, it must be possible to improve the conditions of the kings themselves. Gathering together the remains of the violated pharaohs, the priests transferred them to a series of temporary workshops. The temple of Medinet Habu, administrative headquarters of the royal cemetery housed one such workshop, as did the tomb of Seti I.

Here the priests made valiant attempts to repair the mummies, using modern bandages to conceal the damage caused by the robbers. However, they also took the opportunity to strip the exposed corpses of any remaining highly profitable, officially sanctioned business. The old tombs represented an easily accessible treasury yielding vast quantities of valuable goods which could be recycled or reused.

The rewrapped mummies were replaced in their wooden coffins now stripped of all gold leaf. Both bandages and coffins were labelled and then groups of mummies were stored in convenient chambers dotted about the necropolis. From time to time these groups were inspected and moved, until eventually there was one principal collection of royal mummies housed in the Pinodjem II family tomb at Deir el-Bahari.

Deir el-Bahari, a great natural bay in the eastern face of the Theban mountain, is today best known as the site of Queen Hatchepsut's beautiful mortuary temple. The cliffs behind this temple are honeycombed with private tombs. The masons set to work and soon the tiny entrance to the Pinodjem tomb masked a massive mummy storage depot. A narrow shaft dropped down to a low bent passageway leading to a room some 5 metres (17 feet) square. Here were to be stored the remains of some of Egypt's greatest pharaohs including Ahmose, Tuthmosis I–III, Ramesses I, Seti I and Ramesses II. Beyond this room a taller corridor led to a larger chamber which still held the Pinodjem family burials. The last mummy to be sealed in the tomb was that of Pinodjem II himself. The Deir el-Bahari cache then rested undisturbed for almost three thousand years.

Unfortunately, and in spite of their carefully applied labels, the mummies and their coffins had by now become hopelessly jumbled. The 20th Dynasty King Ramesses IX was now lying in the coffin of the Third Intermediate Period Lady Neskhons, while the coffin of Queen Ahmose Nefertari also yielded the mummy of Ramesses III. Tuthmosis I had been given two coffins, one belonging to Pinodjem I and one of his own coffins, which had been adapted for use by Pinodjem. Pinodjem himself was found lying in a second Tuthmosis I coffin; this had been re-gilded and re-inlaid but subsequently stripped, leaving the name of Tuthmosis once again exposed.

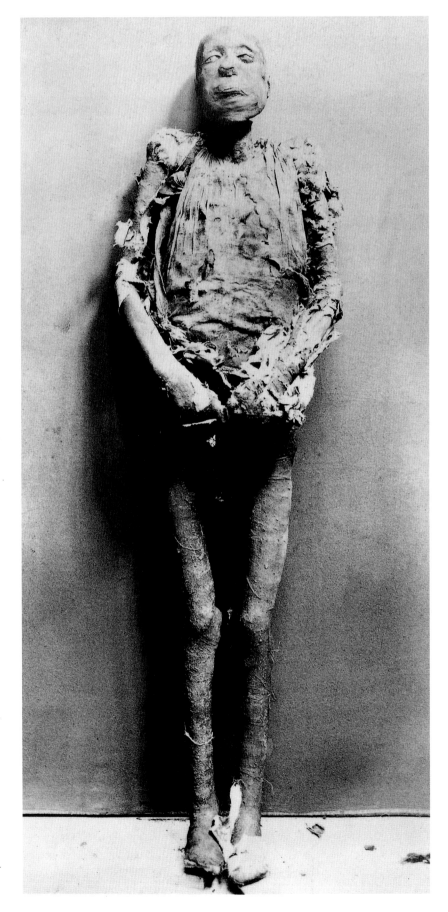

THE HIDDEN KINGS

In 1871 Ahmed el-Rassul, an inhabitant of Qurna village, was searching for a lost goat when he stumbled across the concealed entrance to a tomb. Ahmed rushed home to tell his brothers of his find.

The residents of Qurna had one principal occupation; they stole from the long-dead. Their village was conveniently situated on the edge of the ancient necropolis, with a few of the houses actually built above non-royal tombs. Stealing from the tombs was then, as it had been in the old days and as it still is today, a very serious offence. However, it was also a very lucrative trade. It was all too easy for local "farmers" to search for ancient valuables, and the dealers based in Luxor were always eager for new antiquities to sell to the European tourists who were flocking to Egypt in ever-increasing numbers. Ahmed and his brothers therefore had no thought of informing the authorities of their discovery. Sensing an unparalleled business opportunity they dropped a dead donkey down the shaft. The stink of putrefaction, combined with tales of malevolent ghosts, would be enough to discourage other villagers from taking an interest in the site.

The New Kingdom mummies had no valuables to offer. They had been thoroughly robbed in antiquity by the priests of Amen. After tearing an exploratory hole into the wrappings of Tuthmosis III, Ahmed and his brothers targeted the intact Pinodjem family burials. Slowly, so as not to attract attention and of course lower the price, they released on to the antiquities market an unprecedented series of illustrated funerary papyri and royal shabtis. Thus Ahmed, his brothers and his large extended family grew rich. At the turn of the century an illustrated papyrus could be sold for up to £400, and of course the longer papyri could be cut into two or three sections and sold separately. These pieces, all in good condition and all naming members of Pinodjem's family, made it obvious that one or more Third Intermediate Period royal tombs had been discovered. The question was, where? After ten years of illicit sales,

the Egyptian Antiquities Service decided to launch an investigation.

The activities of the el-Rassul brothers had already come to the attention of the authorities. Their house was searched to no avail, and then on April 6, 1881 Ahmed and his brother Hussein were arrested and sent in chains to Kena, the provincial capital. Here they were interrogated by the governor, the fierce Daud Pasha. In a repeat of the ancient tomb-robber trials the brothers were tortured – beatings on the soles of the feet left Hussein with a permanent limp – but they were able to produce a large number of character witnesses from Qurna. In the absence of any direct proof the trial was abandoned and the brothers were thrown into goal.

Eventually Ahmed and Hussein were released and returned home. Tension in Qurna was, however, running high. Although the case against the brothers was officially not proven, everyone knew that they were guilty and the police mounted a constant watch over the village. The Antiquities Service had already made it clear that they would be launching a new enquiry the following year. The brothers now started to quarrel, and the quarrels soon turned into open fighting. Eventually Mohammed, the eldest brother, decided that the time had come to confess. In return for immunity from prosecution he travelled to Kena and laid the whole matter before Daud Pasha.

On July 6, 1881, Mohammed el-Rassul led a party of officials along the steep mountain path which wound behind the back of Queen Hatchepsut's mortuary temple towards the remote tomb. Emile Brugsch, representing the Antiquities Service, was the first to be lowered down the shaft. Passing through a tiny doorway he shuffled into a low corridor almost blocked by an enormous coffin. Soon this corridor turned to the right away from the light, and here it was possible to stand upright. The corridor led via a short flight of steps to the mummy storeroom. Here, by the flickering light of

his candle, Brugsch saw an amazing sight. The chamber was packed with an unimaginable collection of coffins. It all seemed like a dream.

Their gold covering and their polished surfaces reflected my own excited visage so that it seemed as though I was looking into the faces of my own ancestors ... I took in the situation quickly, with a gasp, and hurried to the open air lest I should be overcome and the glorious prize, still unrevealed, be lost to science.

Brugsch, shocked by what he saw and worried about the risk of fire, rushed from the tomb. Some time later, fully recovered, he made his way past the New Kingdom mummies to discover the burials of the Pinodjem family, which lay in the further chamber. These burials, although looted by the el-Rassul family, were substantially intact.

Brugsch, now in a state of panic and desperately worried about the security of his finds, made what, with hindsight, has to be classed as a remarkably bad decision. No attempt was to be made to record the mummies as they stood. No plans would be drawn, no photographs taken and no list of mummies made. The entire tomb was to be cleared and the mummies were to travel immediately to Cairo. Three hundred workmen were rounded up and set to work. The mummies in their coffins were

ABOVE: THE MORTUARY TEMPLE OF THE FEMALE PHARAOH HATCHEPSUT, DEIR EL-BAHARI.

taken at once from their cool dark tomb, winched up the narrow shaft and laid out to bake in the hot summer sun. Brugsch knew that he had to act fast if he was to preserve his find. Soon, the forty mummies were cocooned in protective matting and sewn into sail-cloth. Within a mere two days the first of the precious cargo was on its way north by boat to Cairo.

News of the find spread rapidly. Along the banks of the Nile crowds gathered to watch as Egypt's ancient kings embarked on their final journey. As the boat steamed by hundreds of peasant women began to weep and tear their hair in the traditional gesture of mourning while their menfolk expressed their respect – and perhaps their regret at the loss of such a rich treasure "stolen" from the peasants by the archaeologists – firing shotguns into the air. In Cairo the customs official taxed with recording the arrival of the unusual cargo was forced to classify the remains as *farseekh*, or dried fish; a description which Herodotus would have well understood.

The mummies' travels were not over. Originally displayed in the Boulak Museum, they were transferred first to Giza, and then to the new Cairo Museum, which opened in 1902. In the 1930s they were moved for political reasons but returned to the Museum soon after. However, there was a growing disquiet over the treatment of Egypt's long dead kings as mere curiosities, and in 1980 President Sadat ordered that the mummy room be closed. Today a selection of mummies may be viewed in the museum. Unfortunately, some of the unnamed mummies, plus that of Pinodjem I, were misplaced and their whereabouts are now, sadly, unknown.

Meanwhile, back in Kena, Mohammed el-Rassul was given a reward of £500 plus a responsible position working for the Antiquities Organization.

REVEALING THE KINGS

Once safely unpacked in Cairo, many of the mummies were subjected to "modern" autopsies conducted as public displays rather than scientific investigations. Tuthmosis III, Egypt's greatest warrior king, was the first to be exposed. His mummy had already been vandalized by the el-Rassuls who, in a vain search for the absent heart scarab, had torn through the wrappings on the left side of the chest. Now the bandages were roughly hacked from his limbs. The mummy thus revealed was in a sorry state with the head, arms, legs and feet snapped off and the penis and testicles missing. This damage had obviously been caused before the mummy was rewrapped by the priests of Amen; someone had incorporated a small broom and two oars into the wrappings to hold the body together.

Tuthmosis III, whose combination of short stature and military prowess have often led to comparisons with Napoleon Bonaparte, had stood 1.6 metres (5ft 3in) tall. His well-preserved face was small and thin, with a narrow high-bridged nose, a low forehead and prominent teeth. The middle-aged king had been almost bald when he died. When re-examined in 1886 his mummy was found to be coated in "a layer of whitish natron charged with human fat, greasy to the touch, fetid and strongly caustic".

The next public unwrapping, held in June 1886, was generally agreed to be a great success. A number of mummies faced the Egyptologists' scalpel, with varying results. The great Ramesses II, unwrapped in a mere 15 minutes, was in good condition: "the eyebrows are thick and white, the eyes are small and close together; the nose is long, thin, hooked like the nose of the Bourbons ...". The head of Ramesses III was disappointingly

coated in thick black resin; the visitors who had watched the unrolling did not stay to see this chipped away with scissors. Queen Ahmose Nefertari, however, had gone bad: "the body was no sooner exposed to the outer air than it fell literally into a state of putrefaction, dissolving into black matter which gave out an unsupportable smell". Her mummy was temporarily buried beneath the museum storehouse; when it was retrieved a few months later the problem had cured itself.

The mummified head of King Seti I is a tribute to the embalmers art. Its calm dignity is that of a man sleeping, rather than dead. Unfortunately, the king's body was less well preserved, with the head snapped off and the abdomen wall badly damaged. Seti had been wrapped with his arms folded over his chest. A "large, heart-shaped mass of stony consistency" found on the right side of the chest seems, indeed, to have been the heart, which must have been displaced during the packing process. Seti's abdomen had been stuffed with resin-soaked linen which had now set hard. His skin turned from dark brown to black soon after it was unwrapped.

One of the mummies discovered in the Deir el-Bahari

RIGHT: KING SIPTAH; EXAMINATION OF HIS MUMMY REVEALED HIS DEFORMED LEFT LEG.

BELOW: THE WELL-PRESERVED HEAD OF KING SETI I; HIS SCARF CONCEALS THE EVIDENCE THAT HIS HEAD WAS SNAPPED OFF IN ANTIQUITY.

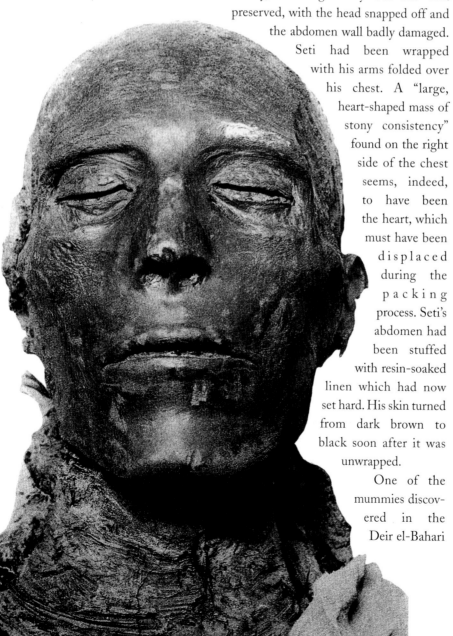

cache proved to have met a horrifying death. Legend already told how, during a period of civil unrest, the southern King Sekenenre Tao had fought against the northern King Apophis. The battle had apparently been sparked by Apophis' unreasonable complaint against the Theban hippopotami were allegedly making so much noise that he was unable to sleep at nights. Now the mummy of Sekenenre Tao shows that he had indeed died a violent death. The king's head had been mortally damaged, with extensive wounds made on more than one occasion by bronze axes. His face, fixed in a horrible grimace, still betrays the agony of his death. The king was presumably mummified quickly, at the site of battle. This may be why his body still emits a foul oily smell.

One other Deir el-Bahari body seems to have met an unnatural, unpleasant end. A rolled sheepskin found in a plain wooden coffin yielded a male body whose face was twisted into an expression of great suffering. The unnamed body had its hands and feet bound, and all the internal organs were intact. Although there had been only a cursory attempt at artificial embalming – traces of dry natron were found on the skin – the dry sheepskin had allowed natural mummification to occur and the skin of the body was relatively well preserved. It seems likely, given its presence in the cache, that this body represents a high-ranking or even royal male. However, the use of sheepskin to wrap the body would have been considered highly disrespectful; the Egyptians never wore animal skins as they were considered unclean. Had the man suffered a horrible death? Perhaps even buried alive, suffocated by his sheepskin shroud?

A SECOND CACHE

In 1898 Victor Loret, inspector of antiquities at Thebes, discovered the tomb of Amenhotep II in the Valley of the Kings. Nervously making his way down the steep dark corridor, lit only by a flickering candle, the Egyptologist came across a horrible sight. A curious wooden boat held "a body lying there upon the boat, all black and hideous, its grinning face turning towards me and looking at me, its long brown hair in sparse bunches around its head. I did not dream for an instant that this was just an unwrapped mummy." The male body which so frightened Loret has been variously identified as either the Pharaoh Sethnakht or the young Prince Webensennu. It had been robbed soon after burial while the resins within the wrappings were still tacky. The thieves had flung the body across the room into the funerary boat, where it had become firmly stuck.

Past this gruesome sight a passageway led downwards to a columned hall that housed an open sarcophagus. Here, in a wooden coffin, lay the

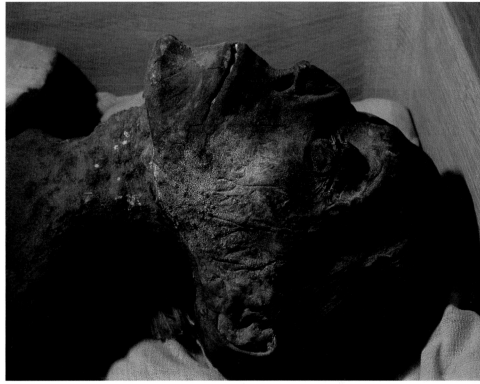

rewrapped mummy of Amenhotep II; at this date the only pharaoh to be found resting in his own tomb. A side chamber yielded three stripped mummies lying side by side, each with a hole in the head and a damaged abdomen. Loret recorded his first impressions of the trio:

ABOVE: THE MUMMY OF AMENHOTEP II WAS DISCOVERED LYING IN HIS OWN TOMB.

> *The first seemed to be that of a woman … her broken arm had been replaced at her side, her nails in the air … Abundant black curled hair spread over the limestone floor on either side of her head. The face was admirably conserved and had a noble and majestic gravity.*
>
> *The second mummy … was a child of about fifteen years … It was naked with the hands joined on the abdomen … The face of the young prince was laughing and mischievous, it did not at all evoke the idea of death. Lastly the corpse nearest the wall seemed to*

LEFT: THE TOMB OF THE PHARAOH SIPTAH WHOSE MUMMY WAS FOUND IN THE 1898 CACHE.

be that of a man ... The face of this person displayed something horrible and something droll at the same time. The mouth was running obliquely from one side nearly to the middle of the cheek, bit a pad of linen whose two ends hung from a corner of the lips. The half closed eyes had a strange expression, he could have died choking on a gag but he looked like a young playful cat with a piece of cloth.

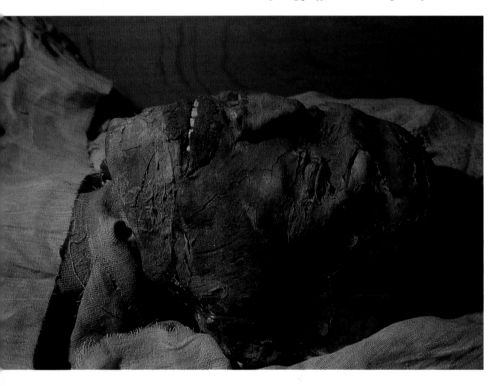

ABOVE: THE MUMMIFIED HEAD OF KING RAMESSES IV.

Loret assumed that the three were members of Amenhotep's immediate family. The unnamed "elder lady" with the plentiful hair is now thought by many to be to be the mummy of Queen Tiy, wife of Amenhotep III and mother of Akhenaten the heretic pharaoh. Other experts believe it to be the remains of Egypt's female King Hatchepsut.

Exploring further, Loret came across a large walled-up side-room that held nine dusty coffins. Bending over to blow away the dust of centuries, Loret revealed a series of royal names. Now the situation became clear: he had discovered a second, smaller royal cache. Here, among others, lay the mummies of Tuthmosis IV, Amenhotep III, Seti II, Siptah and Ramesses IV–VI.

Victor Loret was well aware of the need to keep accurate records of his find. Everything was photographed, detailed plans were drawn and each of the finds – more than two thousand – was meticulously listed. Unfortunately these records were never published, and today all Loret's plans are lost. It took three weeks to pack the tomb contents ready for transportation to Cairo. Then, just as the expedition was about to set sail, a message came from Cairo instructing that the mummies be replaced in the tomb, and the tomb to be sealed.

The wish to conserve Egypt's dead in the dignity of their own tombs is understandable. For the first time the authorities were trying to treat the mummies as dead people rather than ancient curios. Later this decision was revised. The mummies found in the coffins – correctly considered to be intrusive burials – were to be moved to Cairo. Amenhotep II, the prince stuck in the boat, and the three mummies in the side-room – then believed, curiously, to be a part of the original burial, perhaps even human sacrifices – were to be left in the tomb. The mummies were put back exactly as they had been found, the body in the boat being protected from the fingers of curious tourists with chicken wire. Then, disaster struck.

Just a few months after the restoration a gang of thieves managed to outwit – or bribe – the guards and make their way into the tomb. The boat and its prince were stolen, and Amenhotep II was stripped of his bandages. Howard Carter, then working as Inspector General of the Monuments of Upper Egypt, immediately turned detective. He already had a suspect in mind: "I had grave suspicions against Mohammed el-Rassul ... and I watched this man whenever possible, he being a well-known tomb plunderer and his house being quite near the tomb". Discovering the prints of bare feet he photographed the prints before employing a professional tracker to trace the culprit. The tracker followed the prints straight to the house of Ahmed el-Rassul. The footprints eventually proved to be those of Mohammed. Both brothers were subsequently tried for robbery, but once again they were acquitted. The mummy of Amenhotep II was replaced in his tomb but, in 1931, the decision was taken to send the body to Cairo Museum. Amenhotep made his final journey by steam train, apparently travelling in a first class sleeper.

ANIMAL MUMMIES

3

Mummification in ancient Egypt was not confined to human corpses. A vast array of animals, some as carefully embalmed as their human masters, were also accorded this most sacred of rites. However, not all animals were mummified for the same reason.

 ## MUMMIFIED PETS

The ancient Egyptians loved their pets. Cats and dogs and, to a lesser extent, monkeys and geese are often included in the family groups which adorn tomb walls. The pets can usually be found sitting beside their owner's chair. Dogs, often given descriptive names such as "Ebony" or "Good Watcher", were recognized as loyal companions who could also serve as guard and hunting dogs. Cats, much admired for their mysterious, aloof nature, made useful additions to any home. A good cat would ensure that the household was protected against snakes and vermin and could also help in the hunting of marsh birds. At the end of their lives some of these pets were accorded an elaborate funeral; mummified dogs and cats buried in miniature coffins have been found at several archaeological sites. It seems that their grieving owners fully expected to be reunited with their much loved pets in the Afterlife.

LEFT: A WOMAN DRINKS AT THE WATER'S EDGE, SEEMINGLY OBLIVIOUS OF THE LURKING CROCODILE.

BELOW: A WOODEN FALCON-SHAPED COFFIN IDENTIFIES ITS OCCUPANT.

The Valley of the Kings has yielded a number of mummified animals. Amenhotep II even had a pet cemetery situated close to his own tomb. Here three tombs, discovered in 1906, produced a bizarre menagerie of one dog, five monkeys, one baboon, three ducks and one ibis. All the animals had been mummified, and most had been provided with a coffin. All three tombs had, however, been looted in antiquity. In one tomb (now known as KV50) the robbers had entertained themselves by playing with the animal bodies. Theodore Davis was among the first to discover their prank:

I was startled by seeing very near me a yellow dog of ordinary size standing on his feet, his short tail curled over his back, and his eyes open. Within a few inches of his nose sat a monkey in quite perfect condition; for an instant I thought that they were alive, but I soon saw that they had been mummified and that they had been unwrapped in ancient times by robbers ... I am quite sure the robbers arranged the group for their own amusement.

ABOVE: THE GOD THOTH COULD BE DEPICTED AS EITHER A BABOON OR, AS HERE, AN IBIS-HEADED MAN.

The Pinodjem family burial, which formed part of the Deir el-Bahari cache, included the pet gazelle of the Princess Esemkhet. The gazelle had been carefully mummified and encased in a wooden gazelle-shaped coffin so that it could stand upright. However, this was not the animal burial which caused most surprise. A small mummified bundle found in the coffin of the 21st Dynasty Princess Maatkare was at first assumed to be her infant. Both mother and child, it was thought, had died in childbirth. Modern X-ray analysis has since proved the baby to be a young female baboon. This cannot simply be an example of a princess being buried with her pet as examination of Maatkare's body showed that she had indeed died during, or soon after childbirth. Could the baboon have been provided in the coffin as a substitute for her baby who had perhaps survived the birth, or whose body possibly had been lost in the chaos of the embalmer's workshop? This is certainly not the only known example of an animal mummy being passed off as a child. Liverpool University Museum holds a Late Period "baby" mummy which, following X-ray analysis, is now known to be a cat.

The vast majority of animals accorded full burials rites were not domestic pets but living symbols of particular gods. As standards of human mummification declined towards the end of the dynastic era, increasing attention was paid to the mummification of sacred animals. This was not a new idea. Throughout the pharaonic age a multitude of animals, ranging from the small and innocuous (fish, mice, birds even, in one instance, an egg) to the enormous and potentially dangerous (snakes, crocodiles, rams and fully grown bulls) had been embalmed prior to burial in dedicated animal cemeteries. However, during the Late and Graeco-Roman Periods, at a time when Egypt's own idiosyncratic culture was threatened by outside influences, interest in the traditional animal cults and associated animal burials grew.

Many of Egypt's deities were directly associated with animals. Some could even take the physical form of an animal, and so we find Hathor, the mild goddess of motherhood, love and drunkenness, variously represented as a cow, a woman or a cow-headed woman. In her more aggressive alter ego Hathor may also appear as Sekhmet, the lion-headed fury. Thoth, the scribe of the gods, could appear as either a baboon or an ibis. Even those gods who retained a fully human form had their animal emblems; the great god Amen could be represented by the goose or the ram, while his consort Mut was symbolized by the vulture.

These animals, inextricably linked to the gods whom they represented, were imbued with an aura of divinity. At first only a few animals from each species were singled out as divine representatives; a few temple geese may have symbolized Amen within the Karnak precincts, but the overwhelming majority of dynastic geese were bred to be eaten. Gradually, however, the idea took hold until it seems that any animal from a "sacred" class might have its own divine attributes. Now the temples of the gods started to resemble zoos; the temple of Thoth at Hermopolis Magna, for example, was converted into a form of sacred safari park with hundreds of baboons and thousands of ibises wandering freely around, while Sakkara was home to millions of sacred birds.

At death the sacred animals could not be left to rot. They were mummified, bandaged, packed into either miniature wooden coffins or purpose-made pots, and interred in their thousands in the subterranean galleries of the nearby desert cemeteries. It would be hard to overestimate the annual number of animal burials in Egypt; Tuna el-Gebel, the cemetery of Hermopolis, has yielded well over four million ibis mummies. It would appear that during the Late Period over ten thousand ibises were buried each year at Sakkara – a figure high enough to suggest that the priests may have instigated an annual cull.

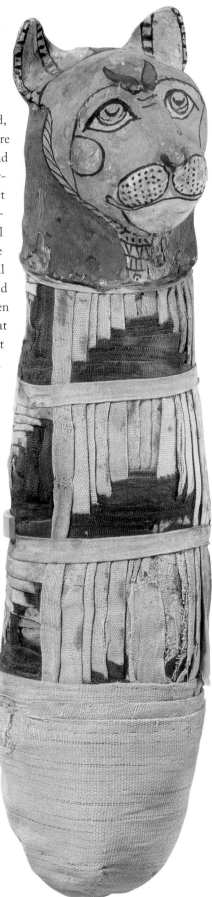

SACRED CATS

The ancient Egyptians are inextricably linked in the public imagination with the worship of cats. Diodorus Siculus tells of one unfortunate Roman who was lynched by an angry Egyptian mob after accidentally killing a cat, while Herodotus has an even stranger cat story:

Whenever there is a fire in Egypt, the cats act in the most peculiar manner. The people allow the fire to burn uncontrolled while they stand in a row and guard these animals which, slipping past the men or leaping over them, run headlong into the flames. When this happens the Egyptians are in deep affliction. If a cat dies in a private house all the inhabitants shave their eyebrows … Cats which have died are taken to Bubastis where they are embalmed and buried …

LEFT: AN ENIGMATIC PACKAGE CONTAINING A MUMMIFIED IBIS.

RIGHT: A DISTINCTIVE LATE-PERIOD CAT MUMMY.

ABOVE: A WOODEN COFFIN IN THE FORM OF A CAT.

Again this apparent cat worship is an over-simplification. Pharaonic cats were not revered for their own sake, although they could always be considered to be the earthly representatives of the cat-headed goddess Bast of Bubastis. Cats were kept as ordinary domestic pets and used as retrievers while hunting in the marshes. It was not until the Late and Graeco-Roman Periods that cat cults grew in popularity. By this time the Bubastis temple was overrun with cats, bred as a lucrative sideline by the priests of Bast.

The pilgrims who flocked to Bubastis had no need to travel with their own dead pet. Here, at the temple, they could select a sacred cat which the priest would kill by breaking its neck. The body would be taken to the temple embalming house where it would be eviscerated, stuffed and bandaged with the legs drawn tight against the body so that the resultant mummy resembled a bulky cylinder topped by a highly naturalistic cat's head. Finally, the neatly wrapped package would be interred, for a fee, in the local catacomb. We do not know how many cats were interred at Bubastis, but the numbers must have run into millions. The comparable cat-based cult at Beni Hassan yielded tons of mummified cats; no one troubled to record or even count the individual bodies, they were simply shovelled up and shipped to England where they were used as fertilizer.

RIGHT: ATTENDED BY HER SERVANT, AN EGYPTIAN WOMAN, GOES INTO MOURNING FOR A CAT.

 # THE APIS BULL

Occasionally, one individual animal from a given species was acknowledged to be the one living representative of a particular god. These representative animals generally belonged to the larger species; rams or bulls. The Apis, a bull with particular markings chosen, like the Dalai Lama, by priests on the death of his predecessor, was celebrated as a living god at Memphis. Here the Apis was sacred in his own right. In life he was revered as a god and a king, with his own palace servants and harem of cows. In death he was given a regal funeral. It is possible that the earliest Apis bulls had been eaten after death, but by the Late Period the bulls were mummified with all due pomp and ceremony.

The sacred bulls had their own place of embalming where the equipment was on a suitably large scale. The massive alabaster embalming tables took the form of low benches whose tops sloped towards a drainage hole. Here evisceration, apparently carried out by injecting liquid through the anus, preceded a period of drying beneath heaps of natron.

When drying was complete the horns and parts of the face were gilded and the bull bandaged in a crouched position. Finally, the animal was placed in a coffin and dragged on a sledge to the Serapeum, the sacred bull cemetery of Sakkara, where a rock-cut gallery linked the individual burial chambers. Here the Apis was interred in a giant sarcophagus.

The Mothers of Apis, the cows who had given birth to the sacred bulls, were also considered worthy of great respect; towards the end of the dynastic period a private smaller-scale cow cemetery was provided for their use, and here they too were mummified before burial. Unfortunately, almost all the Apis burials were destroyed by Christians, intent on stamping out all signs of pagan religious practice.

the CURSE of the MUMMY'S TOMB

4

The boy-pharaoh Tutankhamen died suddenly in January 1323 BC. His own regal tomb was unfinished at his death – no one had anticipated such a tragedy – and, as Egypt plunged into deep mourning, hasty preparations were made to bury the mummified pharaoh in a modest chamber hidden deep within the Valley of the Kings. Here, protected by the prayers and rituals of his priests, Tutankhamen was to rest in peace forever.

MUMMY FEVER

Some three thousand years later Egyptology was the height of European fashion. The Valley of the Kings was silent no longer; it echoed to the sound of mattock and spade as the secrets of the pharaohs were slowly and inexorably laid bare for all to see. Thomas Cook had sent his first boatload of tourists down the Nile in 1840, and soon Luxor, once a sleepy east bank village standing on the site of ancient Thebes, had developed into a bustling holiday resort. By the end of the 19th century the streets of Luxor – now lined with grand hotels – thronged with a mixture of European visitors, amateur Egyptologists and official archaeological missions. All the tourists wanted the same thing; a visit to the west bank necropolis where they could marvel at the colourful tombs and shudder at the pleasingly gruesome mummies. Miss Amelia

ABOVE: THE THOMAS COOK TRAVEL OFFICE SITUATED OUTSIDE THE OLD WINTER PALACE HOTEL, LUXOR.
OPPOSITE: THE GOLD FUNERARY MASK OF TUTANKHAMEN.

Edwards, novelist and soon-to-be founder of the Egypt Exploration Fund (later Society), journeyed to Luxor in the 1873–74 season. She too was keen to witness archaeology in action:

The Boulak (Cairo Museum) authorities keep a small gang of trained excavators always at work in the necropolis of Thebes. These men are superintended by the governor, and every mummy-case discovered is forwarded to Boulak unopened. Thanks to the courtesy of the Governor, we had the good fortune to be present one morning at the opening of a tomb … a mummy case came gradually to light … It gave one a kind of shock to see it first of all lying just as it had been left by the mourners; then hauled out by rude hands, to be searched, unrolled, perhaps broken up as unworthy to occupy a corner in the Boulak collection. Once they are lodged and catalogued in a museum, one comes to look upon these things as "specimens" and forgets that they once were living beings like ourselves. But this poor mummy looked startlingly human and pathetic lying at the bottom of its grave in the morning sunlight.

Miss Edwards was unusual in expressing sympathy towards the deceased. Watching the excavation of the ancient grave had perhaps allowed her to see the mummy as a dead human being. Others were not so thoughtful. In 1895, Henry Morton Stanley recorded his "inventory of articles purchased by a gentleman in the portico of the Ramesseum":

Three men's heads, one woman's head, one child's head, six hands large and small, twelve feet, one plump infant's foot, one foot minus a toe, two ears, one part of a well-preserved face, two ibis mummies, one dog mummy …

The "mummy pits" never failed to disappoint. Wily guides ensured that there would be sufficient mummies to thrill the tourists, even if they had to be imported from other tombs. Visits to Mr Davis' animal tombs were also very popular. Joseph Lindon Smith remembers that children "laughed aloud in their delight" on seeing the lifelike dog mummy standing upright with its eyes open.

The first Egyptian mummy to find its way into the British Museum collection was purchased as a souvenir in 1722. Almost eighty years later Napoleon's troops invaded Egypt. The Louvre benefited by acquiring a collection of intact mummies, while Napoleon and Josephine became the proud possessors of a matching pair of mummy heads, one male and one female. Few respectable tourists would have considered buying a dead body as a memento of a trip to Brighton or Torquay, or displaying a severed English head as a curiosity, but the Egyptian tradition of mummification seems to have confused the moral issue.

The Egyptian dead, long preserved within their dusty bandages, did not resemble the dead of other nations. They were prize specimens, not human remains; a form of natural phenomenon to be dug up, bought, sold, displayed or even thrown away as the owner wished. For many Europeans a genuine mummy, or a mummy fragment, made the perfect souvenir. The fact that dealing in antiquities – and of course in dead bodies – was well known to be illegal, merely added to the thrill of the purchase. Indeed, so great was the demand that some enterprising Egyptians established clandestine mummy

BELOW: AN IMPRESSIVE MUMMY PIT AT THEBES.

factories where they transformed the not-so-long dead into antique looking mummies for sale to gullible Europeans. Horrific tales of "ancient" mummies being recognized as recently vanished Europeans were rife.

Although Miss Edwards could not be tempted to indulge in a defunct Egyptian, her friends did eventually allow themselves to be persuaded:

They bought both mummy and papyrus at an enormous price; and then, unable to bear the perfume of their ancient Egyptian, drowned the dear departed at the end of a week.

Other purchasers are possibly less sensitive. We heard, at all events, of fifteen mummies successfully insinuated through the Alexandrian Custom-house by a single agent that winter. There is in fact a growing passion for mummies among Nile travellers. Unfortunately, the price rises with the demand; and although the mine is practically inexhaustible , a mummy nowadays becomes not only a prohibited, but a costly luxury.

A century later, it was no longer considered particularly "sensitive" to jettison unwanted human remains, no matter how old, in the River Nile.

THE EARLY EXPLORERS

Mummified bodies, although fascinating to the tourists, were of little interest to the professionals. The early Egyptologists were, quite literally, prepared to trample over the dead in an effort to seek out their art, artifacts and writings. Giovanni Battista Belzoni (1778–1823) was very much an archaeologist – many would say treasure hunter – of his time:

The entry or passage where the bodies are is roughly cut in the rocks, and the falling of sand from the upper part or ceiling of the passage causes it to be nearly filled up … After getting through these passages, some of them two or three hundred yards long, you generally find a more commodious place, perhaps high enough to sit. But what a place of rest!

Surrounded by bodies, by heaps of mummies in all directions; which, previous to my being accustomed to the sight, impressed me with horror ... In such a situation I found myself several times, and often returned exhausted and fainting till at last I became inured to it, and indifferent to what I suffered, except from dust; which never failed to choke my throat and nose; and though, fortunately, I am destitute of the sense of smelling, I could taste that the mummies were rather unpleasant to swallow ... When my weight bore on the body of an Egyptian, it crushed it like a bandbox. I naturally had recourse to my hands to sustain my weight, but they found no better support; so that I sunk altogether among the broken mummies, with a crash of bones, rags, and wooden cases, which raised such a dust as kept me motionless for quarter of an hour, waiting till it subdued again ... every step I took I crushed a mummy in some part or other ...

As Belzoni cheerfully admitted: "the purpose of my researches was to rob the Egyptians of their papyri; of which I found a few hidden in their breasts, under their arms, in the space above their knees, or on the legs, and covered by the numerous folds of cloth that envelop the mummy". He reports that the locals, living in the tombs, used pieces of coffin, and even pieces of mummy, to fuel their fires. "It is no uncommon thing to sit down (to eat) near fragments of bones; hands, feet, or skulls are often in the way; for these people are so accustomed to be among the mummies, that they think no more of sitting on them, than on the skin of dead calves".

By the early 20th century, with the development of Egyptology as an academic subject, attitudes had modified. None would now adopt the cavalier approach of Belzoni and his colleagues towards the destruction of antiquities, while human remains were henceforth treated with a degree of respect. However mummies were still not accorded any great value. It was acknowledged that they played a role in the tourist industry, but few Egyptologists took an active interest in mummy studies. Fastidious scholars regarded mummies with distaste – they represented the unfortunate, "popular" side of Egyptology.

TREASURE HUNTING

RIGHT: MISS AMELIA B EDWARDS, FOUNDER OF THE EGYPT EXPLORATION SOCIETY.

The archaeologists in Luxor were now seeking a major archaeological prize: an intact, dynastic royal burial. As they were all too well aware, time was running out. The tombs of many of Egypt's great New Kingdom pharaohs had been found in the Theban necropolis, but none so far had been found intact. Only a few of the kings were now missing. As time went by, and more and more desecrated graves came to light, it became less and less likely that a complete royal burial would ever be found. The treasure hunt grew ever more frenetic.

In 1907 Tutankhamen's embalming cache had been discovered by a team of archaeologists sponsored by Theodore Davis. Two years later a small, undecorated pit tomb was found; the single chamber yielded a few dynastic artifacts including fragments of gold foil bearing the royal names of Tutankhamen and his successor, King Ay. Davis believed this to be the looted tomb of Tutankhamen and, admitting defeat in his search, issued a statement: "I fear that the Valley of the Tombs is now exhausted". This neatly echoed a statement issued by Belzoni almost a century earlier: "It is my firm opinion, that in the Valley of the Kings, there are no more (tombs) than are now known". In fact the small chamber discovered by Davis probably held the remains of a robber's hoard.

In the face of all evidence to the contrary, Howard Carter still believed that the intact tomb of Tutankhamen remained to be found. Carter was trained as an artist rather than an archaeologist. Born on May 9, 1874, the youngest of eleven children of animal painter Samuel John Carter and his wife Martha Joyce, he had come to Egyptology almost by accident. At the age of 17 Carter was employed by the Egypt Exploration Fund as an artist and draughtsman entrusted with inking in the tracings of tomb and temple scenes brought back from Egypt. Later that year, under the patronage of Amelia Edwards, he himself set sail for Egypt where he spent several years copying the monuments and learning the techniques of scientific excavation from Flinders Petrie, the first Egyptologist to apply rigorous mathematical principles to the archaeological dig.

A variety of jobs followed, ranging from Inspector of Monuments to itinerant artist and dealer in antiquities. Carter found himself facing a somewhat uncertain future until one day a mutual friend introduced him to a wealthy amateur Egyptologist, Lord Carnarvon.

Carnarvon had also become an Egyptologist by default. His first passion had been motor cars – he was one of the first to appear before the magistrates for speeding – but a near-fatal crash in 1901 had left him weak and vulnerable to infection. The damp and chill of the British winter was deemed unsuitable for an invalid and his doctors advised him to seek a more amenable climate. In 1903, Lord Carnarvon arrived to spend his first season in Egypt. Egyptology, initially a means of killing time, quickly became his passion. Wealthy enough to fund his own expedition, but lacking the expertise to supervise an excavation, Lord Carnarvon sought an archaeological partner. In 1908 he teamed up with Howard Carter and together the two worked well, digging in the private tombs of Thebes and in the Nile Delta before receiving permission to embark on work in the Valley of the Kings in 1915.

However, by 1921 Carnarvon was losing faith in the project. He had poured a vast amount of money into his excavations, and had seen very little tangible reward. The partners agreed that the 1922–23 season was to be their last.

BELOW: HOWARD CARTER BREACHES A SEALED WALL IN THE TOMB OF TUTANKHAMEN.

A FATAL DISCOVERY?

The story of the discovery of the intact tomb of Tutankhamen is now widely known. On November 4, 1922, a workman employed by Howard Carter uncovered the first of sixteen stone steps leading down to a sealed doorway. Excitedly, Carter telegraphed in code to his patron:

At last have made a wonderful discovery in Valley; a magnificent tomb with seals intact; recovered same for your arrival; congratulations.

Lord Carnarvon telegraphed back: "propose arrive Alexandria 20th", and set sail for Egypt with his daughter, Lady Evelyn Herbert. They reached the Valley of the Kings on the November 23, and the clearing of the stairwell was resumed.

Once the doorway was fully exposed it became possible to read the name of the tomb owner: King Tutankhamen. Unfortunately, it was also now possible to see that the tomb had been opened and re-sealed at least twice in antiquity. Would the tomb prove to be yet another disappointment, thoroughly looted in antiquity? With mounting

tension the workmen dismantled the doorway and cleared the corridor which the Priests of Amen had filled with limestone chips so long ago. By November 26, the excavators were again standing in front of a sealed door. Carter made a small hole and peered inside:

> At first I could see nothing, the hot air escaping from the chamber causing the candle flames to flicker, but presently, as my eyes grew accustomed to the light, details of the room within emerged slowly from the mist, strange animals, statues and gold – everywhere the glint of gold.

Lord Carnarvon was less poetic in his recollection of the momentous occasion:

> Mr Carter, holding a candle before him, put his head in. He did not say anything for two or three minutes, but kept me in rather painful suspense. I thought I had been disappointed again, and I said "can you see anything?" "Yes, yes", he replied, "it is wonderful."

Soon after opening the antechamber Lord Carnarvon, Howard Carter and Lady Evelyn crawled through a small hole into the burial chamber. To their delight this was almost completely filled with an imposing golden shrine inlaid with brilliant blue faience. There was no sign of any forced entry, the original seals were intact, and it seemed that the burial of Tutankhamen was substantially complete within the shrine. However, the antechamber had to be cleared of its treasures before making any attempt to investigate further. The party, sworn to secrecy, crawled back through the hole which was then sealed and concealed for maximum security.

It was to take seven weeks of painstaking work to empty the antechamber. Howard Carter was a methodical worker, well aware of the need to keep accurate records. The process could not be hurried. Each object had to be photographed, pinpointed

ABOVE: LORD CARNARVON AND HOWARD CARTER DISCOVER THE TOMB OF TUTANKHAMEN AT THEBES IN 1922.

RIGHT: THE SCEPTRE OF THE PHARAOH FOUND AMONG TUTANKHAMEN TREASURE.

FAR RIGHT: OPENING THE FOURTH AND INNERMOST GOLD SHRINE, CARTER GAINS ACCESS TO THE SARCOPHAGUS OF THE KING.

ABOVE: THE MUMMIFIED BODY OF THE KING LAY WITHIN A NEST OF GOLDEN COFFINS.

on a plan, described and sketched before it was moved to a storage tomb. Here it was given any necessary conservation treatment and carefully packaged for transfer to Cairo.

It was not until February 18, 1923, that the official opening of the sealed door to the burial chamber took place in the presence of a select invited audience including the Queen of the Belgians and her son, Prince Leopold.

Again, once the shrine was revealed, work moved painfully slowly. It was necessary to clear the room before progress could be made on the dead king, and the fragile shrine proved to be a very tight fit, allowing little room for manoeuvre. The shrine had been built within the tomb, and it had to be dismantled before any progress could be made towards the sarcophagus. Within the outer shrine were three further gilded shrines and a wooden frame holding a delicate linen pall spangled with golden flowers. At last the time had come to unbolt the innermost shrine:

With intense excitement I (Howard Carter) drew back the bolts of the last and unsealed doors; they slowly swung open, and there, filling the entire area within, effectually barring any further progress, stood an immense yellow quartzite sarcophagus, intact, with the lid still firmly fixed in its place, just as the pious hands had left it.

Almost one year after the official opening of the burial chamber, on February 12, 1924, the cracked quartzite lid, weighing a hefty 1.25 tons, was hoisted off the sarcophagus to reveal the outermost of the three golden coffins protecting the mummy. These too had to be opened in order to reach the pharaoh; a time-consuming and delicate process. Finally, on November 11, 1925, the wrapped body was revealed and the autopsy on the dead king could begin under far from ideal conditions within the tomb.

Many academics were faintly disappointed with the contents of the tomb, but few were brave enough to express their reactions in print. Although the burial had yielded hundreds of beautiful artifacts and a multitude of fascinating items of daily use, there was virtually no written material. The lack of textual evidence meant that there was very little to enhance the understanding of late 18th Dynasty political or religious life. This most mysterious of periods in Egyptian history remained an enigma. The man and woman in the street, however, took a very different view.

ABOVE: TUTANKHAMEN'S GOLDEN PECTORAL SHOWING THE VULTURE AND COBRA GODDESSES WHO PROTECTED THE DEAD KING.

NILE STYLE

From the very beginning the general public was absolutely fascinated by the activities within the tomb. Their interest was fuelled by the massive publicity attracted by the find. Each of the major London newspapers dispatched reporters and photographers to Egypt and, even though Lord Carnarvon soon signed an exclusive deal with *The Times*, events in the Valley of the Kings always received detailed front-page coverage. Inevitably, Luxor was swamped with visitors and the expedition was inundated with post. Howard Carter, never a patient man, started to grow exasperated. He did not relish his new found role as public spectacle:

The tomb drew like a magnet. From a very early hour in the morning the pilgrimage began. Visitors arrived on donkeys, in sand-carts, and in two-horse cabs, and proceeded to make themselves at home in the Valley for the day. … There they would sit the whole morning, reading, talking, writing, photographing the tomb and each other, quite satisfied if at the end they could get a glimpse of anything … We were really alarmed sometimes lest the whole wall collapse and a crowd of visitors be precipitated into the mouth of the tomb.

Lord Carnarvon, with his flair for publicity, must take a great deal of the credit – or blame – for Tutankhamen's continuing high profile. He had quickly come to realize the value of his find. Tutankhamen represented money. This was his one chance of recovering the tens of thousands of pounds which he had already poured into Egyptology, and he intended to seize any chance to promote his expedition. His exclusive deal with *The Times* was, with hindsight, well intentioned but naive; it was an attempt to relieve media pressure at the tomb while ensuring that Tutankhamen remained in the public eye at all times. Unfortunately the deal backfired badly, causing a great deal of resentment among the American, British and Egyptian press, who were forced to

resort to increasingly devious means in an attempt to obtain their copy. Denied official access to the tomb, many journalists were not averse to printing speculation and gossip.

Back home, the whole of Britain seemed to have gone Tutankhamen-crazy. Ancient Egypt was all the rage. Everyone wanted to show they had Nile style, and there was an apparently insatiable demand for "Egyptian" clothing, hats, furniture, cosmetics and confectionery. Some items were

BELOW: EGYPTIAN HOUSE-BOATS MOORED IN FRONT OF THE LUXOR TEMPLE.

more tasteful than others: the Tutankhamen-inspired jewellery produced by Cartier and by Van Cleef and Arples was beautiful; however, the Huntley and Palmer biscuit tin fashioned in the shape of a funeral urn and decorated with Egyptian figures was less so. Even the new cinemas were designed with a Nile theme, so that many a traditional town was suddenly presented with a garish replica Egyptian temple on its high street. Egypt had been fashionable before, most notably following Napoleon's 1798 expedition, but never had it had such an effect on everyday life.

Why should the discovery of one relatively minor king have such impact? Sir Leonard Woolley, digging at the Mesopotamian site of Ur (in modern Iraq) throughout the 1920s and 1930s, made a series of spectacular finds including the royal graves, the death pits and even evidence which seemed to prove the Bible story of the Great Flood. And yet Woolley's work, of far greater historical importance than Carter's, passed relatively uncelebrated in the national press. Perhaps the answer lies in part in the accessibility of Luxor. Ur, a remote site known only to a few, lacked glamour. It seemed to belong to another age, the prewar gloom of Bible scholars and antiquarian clergy. Luxor, now a fashionable winter resort, was immediately accessible. Many of those now reading of the spectacular discoveries had already wintered in Cairo, had maybe visited the Valley, and could almost imagine themselves stumbling across a lost tomb. Hundreds more were now inspired to visit Luxor, where they filled the hotels and made Howard Carter's life a misery.

Carter himself suggested that "at the time the discovery was made the general public was in a state of profound boredom with news of reparations, conferences and mandates, and craved for some new topic of conversation". Certainly the timing of the discovery was fortuitous. Europe,

LEFT: AN EGYPT-INSPIRED CARTIER WATCHCASE, BEARING THE IMAGE OF A PHARAOH'S HEAD.

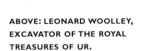

ABOVE: LEONARD WOOLLEY, EXCAVATOR OF THE ROYAL TREASURES OF UR.

needing to forget the horrors of war, was in the mood for something different. There could be no return to the repressed, cluttered and over-elaborate Victorian or even Edwardian style of clothing and furnishing. Ancient Egypt – or rather an interpretation of Egypt – filtered through contemporary artists and designers, offered an alternative of vibrant colours, smoothed outlines and streamlined interiors tinged with a hint of oriental mysticism and, of course, splashes of gold; a new combination of luxury and simplicity which appealed very strongly to the modern postwar generation. However, much of the public interest was undoubtedly stimulated by the spectacular nature of the finds themselves. The discovery of gold in vast quantities has a romantic fascination all of its own. Many were mesmerized by the sheer wealth of the king's possessions; if this was the burial of a minor king, then what treasures would have accompanied a major pharaoh to the Afterlife? some found the day-to-day objects both poignant and compelling, while the mysterious Egyptian gods and goddesses who had guarded the dead king for centuries attracted others. The king's mummy, now disturbed from its long rest and ruthlessly subjected to public scrutiny, excited both interest and compassion. It somehow seemed easy to relate to a king – a boy, young enough to have fought and died in the recent war – who had been buried with his favourite sandals and a lock of his grandmother's hair. Lying within his golden coffin, Tutankhamen did not look like a 3,000-year-old corpse, but instead like a vulnerable young man.

DEATH COMES ON SWIFT WINGS

Lord Carnarvon left Howard Carter to start the laborious task of clearing the tomb. The strain and excitement of the discovery had left him feeling tired, and he set off to enjoy a few days holiday, sailing south to Aswan. Unfortunately, while in Aswan, or just after his return to Luxor, Lord Carnarvon was bitten on the cheek by a mosquito. Soon after, while shaving himself with an ivory handled cut-throat razor, he accidentally cut the scab off the bite. Although he treated the cut immediately with iodine, he developed a high temperature and Lady Evelyn ordered him to bed.

Lord Carnarvon seemed to make a quick recovery but soon relapsed. Deciding to seek further medical advice he travelled with his daughter to Cairo and booked into the Continental-Savoy Hotel. Here he tried to carry on with his life as normal – dining in a restaurant with a colleague and even going to see a film – but his glands were starting to swell and his temperature was again rising dangerously high. Blood poisoning set in, pneumonia soon followed and Lady Evelyn feared the worst.

Lord Carnarvon's weak constitution – the very reason he had gone to Egypt in the first place – was unable to fight the disease. The Cairo newspapers printed daily medical bulletins and Lady Carnarvon arrived from England bringing Dr Johnson, her husband's doctor. Lord Porchester, Lord Carnarvon's son and heir, was hastily summoned from India. At 1.45 am on April 5, 1923 – less than two months after his official entry into the burial chamber of Tutankhamen – the fifth Earl of Carnarvon died. The recorded cause of death was pneumonia.

Lord Carnarvon's body was embalmed in Egypt and then returned to England where it was buried on Beacon Hill. The private funeral was interrupted by the noise of a low-flying aeroplane, chartered by the *Daily Express*. Howard Carter was left to work alone in the Valley of the Kings.

TUTANKHAMEN'S REVENGE

Progress in the Valley of the Kings had until now been slow, with little to interest the packs of journalists still resident in Luxor. Here at last was a dramatic Tutankhamen story which everyone could report. News of Lord Carnarvon's untimely death travelled fast, provoking intense speculation.

Britain, in the aftermath of the First World War and the devastating flu epidemic which followed, was experiencing a wave of interest in all aspects of the occult as the living struggled to maintain some contact with their dead. The old religious certainties and the Christian ban on spiritualism had been swept away. People were now searching for an alternative form of belief which would fill their spiritual void and ease their deep-felt grief.

Seances, automatic writing and ouija boards were more popular than ever before, while Egyptian religion, with its sinister animal-headed gods, curious writings and morbid rituals for the care of the deceased, held a great fascination for many.

Theosophy, an occultic attempt to reach spiritual enlightenment by both intuition and direct communication, was partially inspired by the lost arts and "elementals" of the ancient Egyptians. Once again, it was in vogue.

Jean François Champollion's decoding of hieroglyphics in 1822 had allowed the translation and publication of many Egyptian prayers and spells. These translations were popular with the general public, but they gave rise to a somewhat ill-informed understanding of Egyptian religious beliefs and mortuary practices. Egyptologists did not usually take the trouble to correct public misconceptions. They tended to form a distant, uncommunicative clique involved with their own scholarly work and unconcerned with the more popular involvement in their subject.

Few top class scholars were prepared to waste their time writing popular books and articles. Museums displayed ancient artifacts, but they made

BELOW: A SEANCE; MANY HANDS MADE LIGHT WORK OF CONTACTING THE DEAD.

little attempt to educate the masses. Instead fictional books, plays and later films "taught" Egyptology. And so there quickly developed two distinct levels of understanding of ancient Egypt; the restrained realistic academic version and the non-specialist inaccurate, but highly compelling popular version. There was little, if any, communication between the two.

Tutankhamen's links with Akhenaten, Egypt's heretic pharaoh, made him a particularly suitable study for those interested in the development of Egyptian religion and magic. While Tutankhamen's parentage has never been proved, a great deal of circumstantial evidence points to him being the son of Akhenaten and the Lady Kiya. Akhenaten, the former Amenhotep IV, is today famous for his extraordinary religious beliefs and his distinctive, almost mystical, asexual appearance. These have carried him beyond the narrow field of Egyptology into the world of the occult. Akhenaten attempted to challenge a religious tradition which stretched back to Egypt's prehistoric past, discarding the traditional gods and goddesses in favour of a single deity, the sun-disk or Aten. This experiment failed and the old religion was restored during the reign of his son.

Interfering with a grave – no matter how long dead its occupant – is generally regarded as taboo. Most people believe that the deceased, when buried, should be left to rest and rot in peace and many have an ambivalent attitude to dissection which, while necessary for the advancement of medical science, is rarely considered desirable.

In Britain this attitude stems at least in part from the peculiar history of human dissection which, from the time of Henry VIII, was a recognized punishment for offenders. Hanged bodies would be taken straight from the gallows to the dissecting room, where they would be subjected to unimaginable indignities and denied a proper burial.

A shortage of hanged bodies soon led to the development of black-market body snatching – fresh corpses "resurrected" from the grave and offered for sale to surgeons – and eventually culminated in the passing of the infamous 1832 Anatomy Act. From this time on it was the poor and the destitute who were destined to face the

surgeons knife. Saving for a decent funeral – and thereby avoiding dissection – became a working class obsession, one which has continued almost to the present day.

Howard Carter and his team, seeing themselves first and foremost as scientists, automatically assumed that they had the right to arouse the pharaoh from his slumbers. Carter recognized that "the scientific examinations should be carried out as reverently as possible". The dissection of the mummy seemed to him an entirely natural climax

ABOVE: HOGARTH'S DISSECTING ROOM SHOWS JUST WHY SO MANY FEARED THIS PARTICULAR FATE.

to the opening of the tomb. Not everyone agreed. For the first time Egyptologists had to deal with a public backlash which they had not experienced dealing with looted tombs or isolated mummies.

Tutankhamen had been found more or less as his funeral party had left him, and that made a great deal of difference to the general public. He was recognizably a dead human being. Would Carter and his team be happy if someone attempted to dig up the recently deceased Queen Victoria, asked one *Times* correspondent? Most people agreed that the dead king would not wish to be stripped of his wrappings. Some believed that it might actually be dangerous so to do.

Professor Douglas Derry, the anatomist who unwrapped Tutankhamen's mummy, published a justification of his work, recognizing that "many persons regard such an investigation as in the

LEFT: KING AKHENATEN, OFFERS LOTUS FLOWERS TO THE SUN GOD ATEN.

nature of sacrilege, and consider that the king should have been left undisturbed". Derry argued that, having discovered the body, it was only correct to clear the tomb of its valuables as a wealthy tomb, no matter how well guarded, would undoubtedly be robbed. This, bearing in mind what had happened to the Amenhotep II cache, is probably true.

The same argument applies to the unwrapping of the king, whose person is thus spared the rude handling of thieves, greedy to obtain the jewels massed in profusion on his body.

History is furthermore enriched by the information which the anatomical examination may supply, which in this case in particular was of considerable importance.

ELEMENTAL, MY DEAR ARTHUR

Anyone with a taste for horror fiction already knew just how vindictive an Egyptian mummy could be. A variety of books taught that ancient objects from Egypt could, and often did, have their own unearthly, even fatal, powers. It mattered little that these books were fiction. Many novels involved an intricate tangle of proper names, facts and complete inventions designed to confuse and convince the reader. The curse of the unlucky mummy, the reincarnation of the evil mummy and the power of the tomb owner to reap vengeance on those who despoil the tomb had entered the public imagination and could not be dislodged.

The novelist Marie Corelli had issued a public warning in March 1923, before Lord Carnarvon's death, suggesting that the mosquito bite might have been caused by "the hand of the pharaoh":

I cannot but think some risks are run by breaking into the last rest of a king of Egypt whose tomb is specifically and solemnly guarded, and robbing him of his possessions. According to a rare book I possess … the most dire punishment follows any rash intruder into a sealed tomb.

PHARAOH GUARDED BY POISONS?
LORD CARNARVON WARNED BY MARIE CORELLI.

Miss Marie Corelli sees the hand of a Pharaoh rather than the bite of a mosquito in the illness of Lord Carnarvon.

The novelist, in a letter to the editor of the "New York World," says that she wrote to Lord Carnarvon expressing the wish that nothing unfortunate would chance to him in the pursuit of his discoveries.

She adds:—

"I cannot but think some risks are run by breaking into the last rest of a King of Egypt whose tomb is specially and solemnly guarded, and robbing him of his possessions.

"According to a rare book I possess, which is not in the British Museum, entitled 'The Egyptian History of the Pyramids' (translated out of the original Arabic by Vattier, Arabic professor to Louis XVI. of France), the most dire punishment follows any rash intruder into a sealed tomb. This book gives long and elaborate lists of the treasures buried with several of the kings, and among these are named 'divers secret poisons enclosed in boxes in such wise that they who touch them shall not know how they come to suffer.'

ABOVE: MARIE CORELLI, WHO PREDICTED THE DEATH OF LORD CARNARVON
LEFT: A NEWSPAPER CUTTING QUOTES CORELLI'S CLAIMS.

The almost immediate death of Lord Carnarvon was seen by many as an impressive vindication of Marie Corelli's claim.

Once it became accepted that Tutankhamen had somehow killed Lord Carnarvon, the search was on to find his secret weapon. The idea that his burial might have been protected by a series of poisonous booby-traps is one that has lingered long in the public imagination. It is theoretically possible that the sealed chamber could have housed a deadly cocktail of microscopic spores capable of living for centuries without a host. Indeed, a black fungus was found within the tomb. However, there is no proof that any fatal bacteria or fungus were deliberately buried with the pharaoh, and it is highly unlikely that any Egyptian scientist would have had the knowledge necessary to set such a sophisticated trap.

Ancient Egyptian medicine, although advanced for its time, did not understand the causes of the illnesses which afflicted the population. Bacteria and germs were unknown. While there are those who believe that the ancient Egyptians were capable of harnessing energies which modern science has yet to rediscover – for example, the employment of pyramid-power which some believe can be used to sharpen razor blades, desiccate fish and restore calm to those suffering from the stresses of modern life – these claims have never been scientifically proven. In any case, biological traps would not have been particularly useful to Tutankhamen. The aim of those who guarded the dead was to deter potential robbers, not to kill them months after they had looted the tomb.

As a variant of the theory that the poisoning had been deliberate came the thesis that it was accidental or indirect. Could Lord Carnarvon have been infected by poisonous bat droppings? This would be highly unlikely as there were no bats in the tomb of Tutankhamen. What about the mosquito bite? Could Lord Carnarvon have been infected by a mosquito which had itself been contaminated by Tutankhamen's embalming fluids? asked *The Daily Mail*. There was, however, no water in the Valley of the Kings and therefore, no mosquitoes. The fatal bite must have occurred elsewhere. If Marie Corelli favoured the theory of the hidden poison, others preferred the intangible, long-range curse implemented by spiritual forces or "elementals". The most notable proponent of this idea was Sir Arthur Conan Doyle, the creator of fiction's greatest detective, Sherlock Holmes. Sir Arthur, a man of his times, had developed a great interest in spiritualism and the study of paranormal phenomena. He had already made public his belief in ghosts, fairies, mediums and mystics. As the author of two very popular tales of ancient Egypt – *The Ring of Thoth* and *Lot No. 249* – he qualified as an expert on Tutankhamen's revenge. He gave his opinion on the matter to the *New York Morning Post*:

An evil elemental may have caused Lord Carnarvon's fatal illness. One does not know what elementals existed in those days, nor what their form might be. The Egyptians knew a great deal more about these things than we do.

Asked the obvious question – why had no one else been slain by the curse? – Sir Arthur famously replied: "It is nonsense to say that because 'elementals' do not harm everybody, therefore they do not exist. One might as well say that because bulldogs do not bite everybody, therefore bulldogs do not exist."

Tales of the mummy's curse, or more specifically Tutankhamen's curse, continued to circulate and grow in the telling. Now it was reported as fact that an engraved plaque or clay tablet had warned of the danger facing the archaeologists. The prophecy "Death comes on swift wings to he who disturbs the tomb of the pharaoh" had, it was rumoured, been found carved above the doorway to the tomb. This plaque, which, needless to say, was not

FAR LEFT: TODAY THE BODY OF TUTANKHAMEN STILL RESTS WITHIN HIS GOLDEN COFFIN IN HIS TOMB.

ABOVE: AN ILLUSTRATION FROM *THE RING OF THOTH*, SIR ARTHUR CONAN DOYLE'S TALE OF ANCIENT EGYPT.

included among Howard Carter's meticulous inventory, was apparently being suppressed by the excavators who were frightened by its message.

A second warning was, allegedly, engraved on a golden torch at the entrance to the treasury within the tomb. This torch does exist, and it is indeed engraved with a spell, but the spell is innocent. Rumour maintained that the last line "… I will call all those who cross this threshold into the sacred precincts of the King who lives for ever", had been erased by Howard Carter, again to prevent panic spreading among the workforce.

The ancient Egyptians certainly believed in the power of magic. Committing a spell to writing was known to make it stronger. Did the deceased ever attempt to protect their tombs with curses? The answer appears to be an emphatic no. The magic connected with the rituals of death was overwhelmingly intended to protect the deceased against any mishap on the way to the Afterlife, rather than against any physical invasion of the tomb. It focuses on the fate of the mummy, rather than on the future tomb robber. Very occasionally, and only during the Old and Middle Kingdoms, tombs were inscribed with a warning which some have interpreted as a curse: "As for any person who would enter this tomb unclean and do something evil to it, there will be a judgement against him by the Great God". These warnings make it clear that it was not the deceased, but the Great God, who would mete out the appropriate punishment. No such warning was found in Tutankhamen's tomb.

It is perhaps telling that the Egyptians themselves, those who would have had the greatest understanding of the powers of the ancient magic, were not averse to looting the tombs of their ancestors. They clearly had no fear of violating the tomb, and no horror of the mummy's curse. The ancient Egyptians did believe in ghosts, but they did not believe in reincarnation.

BELOW: AN ILLUSTRATION FROM A 1934 NEWSPAPER DEPICTS A DISTRESSED TOURIST, LOST IN THE TOMB OF RAMESSES, CALLING OUT TO THE DEAD KING FOR HELP TO FIND HER WAY.

LIES AND STATISTICS

On April 6, 1923, the *Daily Express* printed a story telling how, at the instant of Lord Carnarvon's passing, all the lights in Cairo were extinguished; apparently no explanation could ever be found for this unexpected power failure. Power cuts in Cairo are, however, by no means rare.

Far more intriguing was the story of Lord Carnarvon's three-legged fox terrier bitch, Susie, who had been left behind in England. At exactly the moment of her master's death, Susie apparently sat bolt upright and howled. In later versions of the story, the dog actually died.

In 1934 the American Egyptologist Herbert Winlock attempted to disprove the theory of the curse by studying the statistics. He found that six of the 26 people present at the opening of the tomb had died within ten years, while only two of those who had been present at the lifting of the sarcophagus lid had since died. Most telling of all, of those who had first crept into the burial chamber, only Lord Carnarvon – a man who was known to be in ill health – had died prematurely. The man most responsible for the violation of the king's privacy, Howard Carter, died on March 2, 1939, aged 64, some 16 years after his patron, while Lady Evelyn did not die until 1980. Professor Derry, who conducted the king's autopsy, reached the age of 87.

The curse victims certainly seemed to have been chosen in a random fashion. As might be expected, the majority were found to have died of natural causes. However, one violent death attributed to Tutankhamen was that of Professor H G Evelyn White, lecturer at Leeds University, who committed suicide in a taxi cab. The newspapers were thrilled to learn that the Professor had left a suicide note stating: "I know there is a curse on me". A second violent death was that of the Egyptian Prince Ali Fahmy Bey, a tourist visitor to the tomb, who was later murdered by his wife. Strangest of all was the death of the Hon. Richard Bethell, a private collector and assistant to Howard Carter, who was found dead of natural causes at the Bath Club in 1929. Soon after hearing the sad news his aged father, Lord Westbury, the owner of a small collection of Egyptian antiquities, threw himself out of seventh-storey window. On the way to the cemetery Lord Westbury's hearse ran over and killed an eight-year-old boy.

Of course the death, or indeed the misfortune, of any archaeologist could be interpreted as the mummy's revenge. Curse theorists studied the lives of the great Egyptologists in an attempt to validate their case. Some unusually long-lived curse victims have been identified in the popular press. Heinrich Brugsch (1827–94) was apparently given to schizophrenic tendencies by the curse; Jean François Champollion (1790–1832) apparently died as a result of decoding hieroglyphics; Flinders Petrie (1853–1942) was apparently killed because of his

ABOVE: HOWARD CARTER AND LORD CARNARVON AT THE ENTRANCE TO THE TOMB OF TUTANKHAMEN.

interest in the pyramids. Even Giovanni Battista Belzoni, who died of dysentery while travelling to Timbuktu, has been included among the victims.

Howard Carter would have nothing to do with the curse. Interviewed by the *New York Times* he made his feelings plain:

He said that he had not the slightest belief that any occult influence was responsible for the death of Lord Carnarvon, and that he had no fears for himself in that direction. "It is rather too much to ask me to believe that some spook is keeping watch and ward over the dead Pharaoh, ready to wreak vengeance on anyone who goes too near", Carter said.

Later he seems to have abandoned any attempt at subtlety: "The answer is spherical and in the plural" is possibly an apocryphal response taken out of context; "and by the way I am still alive" seems more convincing. He categorically denied any superstitious tales, and as for the idea that the tomb might be booby-trapped with dangerous spores or poisons, he always maintained that there was no place safer from risk as "scientific research had proved it to be sterile".

STRANGE HAPPENINGS

Not all Egyptologists were keen to dismiss the curse theory. At least one had a vested interest in keeping it well and truly alive.

Arthur Weigall, one time Inspector of Antiquities at Thebes, had returned to Luxor as the special correspondent of the *Daily Mail* to report on the Tutankhamen discoveries. As an ex-colleague, Weigall expected Carter and Carnarvon to allow him access to privileged information denied to the other journalists. The fact that he was not given any special treatment, and indeed was barely recognized as a fellow archaeologist, caused him to develop a grudge against both the tomb and its excavators. It seems that Howard Carter, already harassed by bevies of journalists, regarded Weigall as something of a traitor to the Egyptological cause.

It is from Arthur Weigall's 1924 book *Tutankhamen and Other Essays* that we learn the curious story of the cobra which ate the golden song-bird. Howard Carter, anticipating a lonely season in the Valley of the Kings, had arrived at Luxor with a canary in a gilded cage. The workmen were fascinated; they had never heard such a creature, and they decreed that the bird was an omen of great luck. When Tutankhamen's tomb was discovered soon after, they named their greatest find: "The Tomb of the Golden Bird". However one day, while Howard Carter was travelling to meet Lord Carnarvon, a cobra squeezed between the bars of the cage and ate the canary. Good luck had turned to bad and it seemed particularly relevant to Weigall that it was a cobra – the very snake which featured on the royal headdress – which had silenced the bird.

Weigall, whose income depended on the popularity of his books and journalism, told a series of sinister tales cleverly calculated to appeal to those interested in the Egyptian occult. His own opinion of the curse was strategically vague: "I have heard the most absurd nonsense talked in Egypt by those who believe in the malevolence of the ancient dead; but at the same time, I try to keep an open mind on the subject". It seems that Weigall wished to alienate neither his former colleagues nor his potential readers. He did, however, refute the suggestion that a curse had been found to exist within the tomb.

Weigall's most mysterious story concerned a cat, an animal which carries its own mystical connotations. He told how Lord Carnarvon, excavating in 1909, had discovered the hollow wooden statue of a large black cat housing a cat mummy. By some mischance this piece had been left in Weigall's bedroom and he was fully aware of its presence as he prepared for sleep: "… the moonlight which now entered the room through the open French windows fell full upon the black figure of the cat; and for some time I lay awake watching the particularly weird creature as it stared past me at the wall". In the dead of night Weigall was jerked awake by a loud crack like the firing shot of a pistol. The cat coffin had split in two to reveal a mummified cat, the bandages torn around its neck. At the same time a large grey cat sprang towards Weigall's bed and inflicted a painful scratch on his hand.

A second tale concerned the mummified body of a priest. This particular mummy, within its coffin, made Weigall feel strangely uncomfortable even though he was accustomed to dealing with mummies. Eventually he decided to unwrap the body to gaze at the dead priest's face. The mummy was unwrapped, recorded and photographed, and the old bandages were taken into the house for

LEFT: SACRED CATS FEATURED HEAVILY IN TALES OF THE EGYPTIAN SUPERNATURAL.

OPPOSITE: TUTANKHAMEN'S EARLY DEATH IS APPARENT IN THE YOUTHFUL PORTRAIT ON HIS MUMMY MASK.

study, while the exposed body was left outside. Soon afterwards a young child in the house was taken violently ill; only when the mummy and its wrappings were dispatched to Cairo did the child recover. This was not the end of the matter "… when, a month or two later, I developed the

photographs which I had taken of the unwrapped body, there, between it and my camera, stared a shadowy face". As Weigall himself pointed out, it was quite possible that he had taken two exposures on the same plate. However, could the face have a more sinister explanation?

RESURRECTED

As the magical powers of ancient Egypt made their way into popular culture, reincarnated Egyptians started to surface. One of the most persuasive was "Ivy B.", also known as Rosemary, a so-called writing medium who identified herself as the modern representative of the 18th Dynasty "Princess Telika" or "Nona" – a daughter of the king of Babylon and married to the great pharaoh Amenhotep III. Mrs B., who started speaking her version of ancient Egyptian in 1927, was able to confirm the supernatural powers of the ancient priests who she claimed were able to use telepathy and tell their own future. Many Egyptologists were

wearily familiar with such reincarnations; already a French gentleman had written to Howard Carter to reveal himself as the Emperor Tut-ank-Hamon.

Most famous of all, and a good friend to many Egyptologists, was Dorothy Louise Eady, better known as Omm Seti. Dorothy believed herself to have lived an earlier life as Bentreshyt, a slave girl made pregnant by Seti I. From the age of fourteen onwards she apparently received regular nocturnal visits from the pharaoh, who appeared both as a mummy and as a man. Dorothy moved to Egypt in 1933 and spent her later years living at Abydos, home of the Seti Temple, where she died in 1981.

DANGEROUS SOUVENIRS

Tales of the mummy's curse spread, causing a general unease. People started to worry about the Egyptian objects – both genuine and fakes – in their own private collections. Could their fake faience cat actually come alive? How dangerous was their mummified hand? Fearful, people resorted to desperate means. Some buried their unwanted antiquities in their gardens, or threw them into rivers, creating a problem for the archaeologists of the future. The British Museum found itself inundated with parcels housing a variety of Egyptian souvenirs and mummified body parts; few of the parcels gave any return address. Most of the pieces, found to be worthless, were thrown away. None, as

far as is known, ever caused any member of the museum staff any harm.

To this day there are some who maintain that the British Museum holds a cursed coffin lid in its collection. This innocent piece is supposed to cause harm to those who offend it and has been blamed for a variety of disasters including the sinking of the *Titanic*. Arthur Weigall, of course, claimed to know the full history of the unfortunate coffin and could confirm that its former owner had lost an arm soon after purchasing it. The lid – known to believers as the coffin of the magical priestess of Amen-Re – is in fact an ordinary 21st Dynasty coffin lid belonging to an unnamed lady.

OPPOSITE: THE *TITANIC* – COULD HER FATE HAVE BEEN THE RESULT OF AN EGYPTIAN CURSE?

STAR *of* PAGE *and* SCREEN

GOTHIC SCRIPTS

We should not be surprised to find that the mummy is a frequent visitor to the pages of the gothic horror story. A well-preserved corpse, still recognizably human, although some thousands of years old, can inspire the most frightening of tales. While some mummy stories can most kindly be described as "penny dreadfuls", others are tightly crafted and full of accurate Egyptological facts which allow the discerning reader to suspend belief and wallow in the tale of the supernatural. Even eminent Egyptologists have been known to enjoy reading these stories; some will even admit to their weakness in print. It is perhaps inevitable – and a tribute to the more successful writers – that less discerning readers, convinced by the use of recognizable Egyptian names and locations, have tended to interpret fiction as fact.

The popularity of the mummy story undoubtedly influenced public reaction to the discovery of Tutankhamen's tomb and the sudden death of Lord Carnarvon. Theophile Gautier's highly popular *The Romance of the Mummy*, published in 1857, had set the scene by telling the highly plausible tale – or prophecy – of the discovery of an intact tomb in the Valley of the Kings by the English Lord Evandale and Dr Rumphius, his hired archaeologist companion. The tomb, however, was not that of a young king and Everdale

proved to be no Carnarvon. Evandale and Rumphius had stumbled across the burial of a beautiful queen whose "fine hands and feet, with nails of polished agate; the cup of the breasts, small and pointed; the swelling of the hip and thigh" captivated Lord Evandale forever.

Edgar Allen Poe's 1845 *Some Words with a Mummy* had involved "an experiment or two with the Voltaic pile" – rejuvenating the mummy by means of electricity, thus highlighting the possibility of resurrecting the dead by scientific means. Poe's mummy is surprisingly polite under the circumstances; raised from his eternal rest he answers a series of questions about his past life and the tale ends with the author contemplating his own mummification.

It was left to Bram Stoker to inject realistic horror into the tale. Stoker had published *Dracula*, his story of the vampire Count, in 1897. *Dracula* was a steady success but certainly not a best seller. The novelist was forced to continue writing horror stories; *The Jewel of Seven Stars* – a mummy story similar in style and plot to *Dracula* – followed in 1903; *The Lady of the Shroud* – a tale of suspected vampirism – was published in 1909; *The Lair of the White Worm* was his final novel published in 1911. *The Jewel of Seven Stars* told the tale of the Egyptian Queen Tera, whose unwrapping and

resurrection in a lonely house in Cornwall led to a predictably unpleasant ending for all concerned.

The most recently acknowledged mistress of the mummy tale is Anne Rice, whose gothic novel *The Mummy* (1989) tells the story of Ramses (Ramesses) II, or Ramses The Damned. Through his own actions, Ramses has become an immortal; his tragedy is that he can never die. Awakened from a centuries-long sleep and transported from Egypt to the London home of an eminent archaeologist, he sets out on a quest to find his one true love. This, of course, leads to unforeseen violence and death before Ramses recognizes where his heart really lies. Like Rice's charming vampires, Ramses proves to be a handsome and sophisticated pharaoh, a man of great sensuality, if perhaps little common sense. Ramses is not, however, a true mummy. He has never died, nor been eviscerated and embalmed, and his brain remains intact.

ABOVE: ANNE RICE, MISTRESS OF THE MODERN MUMMY GENRE.

THE MUMMY IN FILM

The undead have always been a staple of gothic horror films. The mummy – not dead, not even decomposing, just sleeping – provides a welcome and exotic variant on the ever-popular vampire or resurrected corpse theme, allowing mummy-based gothic to develop into a movie sub-genre in its own right.

In many ways mummies make life easy for the film makers. Mummies come complete with their own natural aura of mysticism and faint menace so that cinema audiences, familiar with the mummies in museum collections, are already half inclined to believe that the worst could happen and the dead could live. They understand that the mummy, just like the vampire, can be released from death by magic and there is therefore no need to fall back on the mad scientists, radiation leaks, chemical sprays and visitors from outer space which feature so heavily in the more scientific horror films. A simple spell – often recited by accident – the application of a secret potion, or even the innocent burning of incense, will always do the trick.

The ancient tomb offers a different, more exotic, setting to the traditional dark and lonely graveyard, while the Egyptologist's study and the dusty museum provide suitably claustrophobic atmospheres where the true horror of a situation can develop. The opportunity to explore the ancient Egyptian occult is a bonus, allowing a new twist to the fear. This occultic aspect of the vampire tale, once considered very important, now tends to be understated: some of the Hermetic symbolism which so fascinated the Theosophists was included in the original *Dracula* illustrations, but these were dropped from the stage and screen interpretations.

However, as the star of a film, the mummy comes with in-built limitations which ultimately make it less successful than the vampire. Although Bram Stoker's original *Dracula* was no gentleman, he quickly mutated into a handsome, debonair, sophisticate whose intimate biting of the throat was charged with sexual tension. Dracula, chief

OPPOSITE: THE MUMMY ARISES FROM THE TOMB.

among vampires, has been interpreted on many levels; as a tale of Victorian sexual frustration, as man's fear of woman; as a Christian fable or even as a feminist myth. Told and retold from various angles, vampire tales and films have remained ever popular.

By contrast, the celluloid mummy, once aroused, is a less than subtle being. Covered in rotting bandages, unable to speak or see and probably foul-smelling, he or she is no sophisticated tool of horror. This is to a large extent the fault of the mummy costume. In the *Wolf Man* and, to a lesser extent, *Frankenstein*, the actor can barely be seen beneath the make-up. There is little opportunity to reveal any real acting skill and the mummy – an animated mass of bandages – lacks charisma. Resurrected killer mummies may be frightening,

but only in the way that an animated corpse, zombie or robot inspires fear. A mummy scene which seems menacing on the printed page can all too easily appear ridiculous on the stage or screen.

Only those mummies who can successfully shed their bandages and expose their flesh and feelings can fully engage our sympathies in the way that Dracula does. The most compelling mummies in film and literature are not true mummies at all; those who have undergone the full embalming process, with lungs, brain and intestines removed, tend to be resurrected as unthinking, zombie-like creatures. Films featuring these characterless mummies tend to focus on the machinations of the attendant priests and archaeologists, relegating the mummy itself to the role of a killing machine.

A BRIEF HORROR HISTORY

The 1920's and 1930's – the era of Tutankhamen-mania – was the age of the classic horror film. Boris Karloff, Bela Lugosi and Lon Chaney were stars, Tod Browning and James Whale were directos and Carl Laemmle was a producer at Universal Studios. *Dracula* (1930), *Frankenstein* (1931) and *Dr Jekyll and Mr Hyde* (1932) were great commercial successes. At the same time escapist tales of the exotic Orient were becoming popular with cinema audiences: *The Sheik*, starring Rudolph Valentino was released in 1920, and Cecil B de Mille's *The Ten Commandments* opened in 1923. Mummy films, combining the contemporary fashions of horror and ancient Egypt, were bound to succeed.

The Mummy (1932), based on *The Ring of Thoth* by Sir Arthur Conan Doyle and starring Boris Karloff in the title role, was seen as a natural successor to *Dracula*. There had been earlier mummy films – Theophile Gautier's short story *The Mummy's Foot* had been filmed in 1902 as *The Haunted Curiosity Shop*, while in 1911 there had

RIGHT: RAMESSES II, FATHER OF ALL FILM MUMMIES AND THE FACE THAT LAUNCHED NUMEROUS INTERPRETATIONS.

ABOVE: ABBOT AND
COSTELLO'S 1955
ENCOUNTER EXPLOITED THE
HUMOROUS POSSIBILITIES
OF THE TOMB.

been three films, each imaginatively called *The Mummy* – but this was the first time that the mummy had starred in a major studio production. Karloff played the priest Imhotep who, having been buried alive in ancient Egypt, is brought back to life by an innocent archaeologist reading aloud from a magical papyrus. The revived Imhotep, now disguised as the Egyptologist Ardath Bey, recognizes the reincarnated spirit of his long lost love. Unfortunately her spirit is already occupying another living body and Imhotep is forced to plot the death of the beautiful Helen Grosvenor. Imhotep is shown to be a humane, if ruthless, mummy. The cinema audience is invited to sympathize with his dilemma and to understand his compulsions. The revived mummy seeking his lost love was to become a popular theme.

At the time of filming it was claimed that the appearance of *The Mummy* was based on the body of Seti II, a badly damaged mummy which had been restored in antiquity and stored in the Amenhotep II cache. However, it would seem that the

BELOW: VALERIE LEON IN
*BLOOD FROM THE MUMMY'S
TOMB*, SHOWING THAT SOME
CINEMATIC EGYPTIANS
WERE BETTER PRESERVED
THAN OTHERS.

make-up artists were equally inspired by the distinctive mummy of Ramesses III, who influenced almost every subsequent film mummy. This body , recovered with the Deir el-Bahari cache, had been neatly wrapped; his arms were flexed across the chest and his hands were fully extended rather than clenched so that his palms touched his shoulders. His head, exposed during the 1886 public unwrapping, was well preserved with artificial eyes beneath the eyelids. Unfortunately the head had become detached from the body and photographs showed his neck draped with a fold of linen to conceal the break. This inadvertently sparked a fashion for scarves and collars among film mummies.

The Mummy generated a minor wave of moderately successful films: *The Mummy's Hand* (1940), *The Mummy's Tomb* (1942), *The Mummy's Ghost*

(1944) and *The Mummy's Curse* (1945). Eventually, having reached the end of the line, Universal produced *Abbot and Costello Meet the Mummy* (1955).

A new gothic revival occurred in the late 1950s. In America, television showed the great horror movies and developed a youthful cult following. In Britain, Hammer Films reinterpreted the classics of gothic cinema, including *The Curse of Frankenstein* (1957), *Dracula* (1958), *The Hound of the Baskervilles* (1958) and *The Mummy* (1959). *The Curse of the Mummy's Tomb* (1964) and *The Mummy's Shroud* (1967) followed, while Bram Stoker's *The Jewel of Seven Stars* was adapted twice, appearing as *Blood from the Mummy's Tomb* (1971) and *The Awakening* (1980). By now pure gothic horror seemed to have run its course and subsequent films veered away from the traditional storyline.

Included among the deviant mummy films must be *Blood Feast* (1963), a violent film about a madman's attempts to resurrect an Egyptian princess by dismembering nubile girls. Other obscure mummy movies include *Dawn of the Mummy* (1981), *Time Walker* (1982) and *The Tomb* (1985). *Time Walker* features a mummy from outer space while *The Monster Squad* (1987) has an unravelling mummy among the monsters of the title. *The Abominable Dr Phibes* (1971), while not a mummy film in the strict sense, certainly offers a new slant on the horrors of the pharaonic age. In this kitsch film Dr Phibes, played by Vincent Price, disposes of his victims by replicating the twelve plagues of Egypt.

BELOW: *THE MUMMY'S TOMB* (1942); AN ATTRACTIVE YOUNG WOMAN GIVEN TO SCREAMING WAS AN ESSENTIAL ACCESSORY FOR EVERY SUCCESSFUL MUMMY.

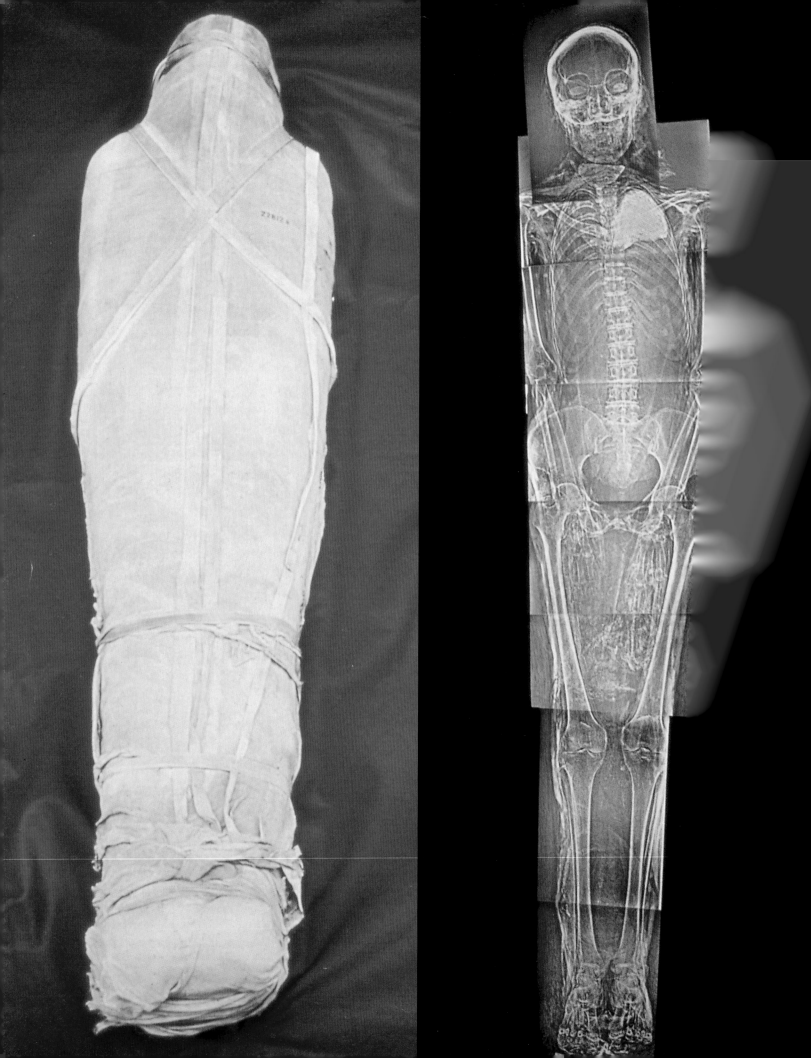

UNWRAPPING
the MUMMY

 MUMMY MEDICINE

Throughout the early days of medicine there was a lingering confusion between *mummia*; the rare and fantastically expensive health-enhancing bitumen believed to seep from the Persian mountains, and mummies; cheap, readily available, long-dead Egyptians. Perhaps this is why for centuries ground-up human mummy was regarded as an invaluable form of medication.

The Greek Dioscorides (40–90 AD) and the Persian Avicenna (980–1037 AD) had both recommended mummy as a general cure-all, effective against a diverse variety of ailments ranging from nausea and vertigo to paralysis.

First prescribed by the Medieval doctors of Alexandria, word of the wonder drug soon spread westwards. By 1657 *The Physical Directory* included the hybrid "*mummia*, a thing like pitch" which, it cautioned, some believed to be extracted from ancient tombs. Mummy was now included in all the best medicine chests.

The black powdered mummy could be mixed with herbs and ingested with water; when boiled into an ointment or mixed with grease it made a useful external treatment for bruises, wounds and sores. Not surprisingly, mummy was in great demand. Catherine de Medici and Frances I of France, who took his mummy mixes with rhubarb, were perhaps the most prominent advocates of the Egyptian wonder-drug, with the queen sending her

own chaplain to Egypt to ensure her private supply.

Now mummies were being sought out and destroyed in the name of medicine. A remarkable trade developed with large numbers of ancient Egyptians being shipped from Alexandria to Europe. The supply of genuine mummies was, however, somewhat dubious, and enterprising tradesmen manufactured their own "ancient" mummies recycling the newly dead – often executed criminals or the poor, diseased and destitute – whose unwanted bodies, suitably bandaged, coated in pitch and buried for a couple of years, could be made to resemble the mummies of their ancestors.

The genuine ancient mummy could be recognized by its perfume – it should not smell of pitch – and by its powdery consistency, but not everyone could tell a genuine from a fake. Not surprisingly, many of the patients treated with mummy powder developed severe stomach cramps and nausea! Ambrose Pare, a prominent French physician, had

ABOVE: AVICENNA
INSTRUCTS HIS STUDENTS
IN THE MYSTERIES OF
EASTERN MEDICINE.

OPPOSITE: X-RAY ANALYSIS
REVEALS THE BODY WITHIN
THIS TIGHTLY WRAPPED
21ST DYNASTY MUMMY.

already warned against "this wicked kind of drogge" which was likely to injure the health. John Webster seemed to agree:

> *Your followers*
> *Have swallowed you like mummia, and being sick*
> *With such unnatural and horrid physic*
> *Vomit you up i' th' kennel.*

The White Devil (1612), Act 1 Scene 2

During the 18th century this distasteful trade was brought to an abrupt halt when the Turkish rulers of Egypt – suspecting some obscure Christian plot requiring a constant supply of long-dead bodies – imposed a heavy tax on the mummies. However, it was not until the early 20th century that Thebans stopped applying a mixture of genuine mummy powder and butter to bruises.

By the 19th century some other ingenious uses had been developed for what must have seemed like a never-ending supply of mummies. The mummy itself could be incorporated as an ingredient in bituminous "mummy brown" oil paint. Its discarded linen bandages could be exported to the USA, where for a short time mummy linen was made into brown paper used to wrap food. An unfortunate cholera epidemic – almost certainly not caused by ancient dynastic infection – caused a public outcry and paper manufacture was halted.

The burning of mummies to provide both light and heat was already well established in Egypt; Wallis Budge has described how Late Period mummies, coated in resin "break with a sound like the cracking of chemical glass tubing, they burn very freely and give out great heat". There was even a rumour, spread by Samuel Clemens (a.k.a. Mark Twain) that mummies were used to fuel the Egyptian locomotives.

BENEATH THE BANDAGES

Amateurs and professionals alike felt a great desire to know what lay beneath the neatly wrapped bandages of the mummy. There was only one certain way to find out.

The earliest known public unwrapping, or "unrolling", was performed by the French consul in Cairo in 1698, while in 1718, Christian Hertzog had unrolled a mummy and published a brief record of his finds before grinding and selling the hapless corpse as powdered *mummia*. In 1814, the Champollion brothers unwrapped a young male mummy dating to the Ptolemaic period. The first series of scientific unrollings – unwrappings performed in order to enhance knowledge rather than to entertain the general public – was conducted by the German anthropologist Johann Blumenbach (1752–1840). Blumenbach unwrapped at least seven human and animal mummies in England, keeping detailed notes of his work. He was disappointed to find that many of the ancient mummies held in private collections were in fact modern fakes, mass produced for the tourist market.

It was the London surgeon Thomas Joseph Pettigrew (1791–1865), physician to the Duke of Kent, who was to turn unrolling into an artform Pettigrew had already assisted the great Giovanni Battista Belzoni in his public unwrapping of mummies. As a former circus strongman, Belzoni knew a good attraction when he saw one. His 1821 recreation of a pharaoh's tomb, held appropriately enough in the Egyptian Hall, London, had proved a great success, inspiring Horace Smith to flights of dubious verse:

An Address to the Mummy in Belzoni's
Exhibition
Speak! for thou long enough hath acted dummy,
Thou hast a tongue – come, let us hear its tune:
Thou'rt standing on thy legs above ground,
Mummy!
Revisiting the glimpses of the Moon.
Not like thin ghosts or disembodied creatures,
But with thy bones and flesh and limbs and
features.

The exhibition opened with the public unrolling of both a human mummy which was found to be "perfect in every part", and a mummified monkey. After a year it closed – Belzoni's lease had expired – and the contents of the "tomb" were auctioned off. Lot 15 was a mummy: "When unfolded before Physicians, the Liver etc., was found among the foldings over the lower part of the Stomach, and will be delivered to the purchaser".

Fascinated by Belzoni's work, Pettigrew started to purchase his own mummies – in the early 19th century a mummy could be bought for less than 25 US dollars – so that he could perfect the art of unrolling in private. His first public unrolling occurred on April 6, 1833, at Charing Cross Hospital. This proved to be a great success with demand for tickets running high. Subsequent unrollings saw the Archbishop of Canterbury and the Bishop of London unable to obtain tickets – they were asked to leave as Pettigrew lectured and then unrolled a mummy at the Royal College of Surgeons. Of course, despite meticulous preparation,

Pettigrew could never guarantee that there would be a well-preserved body beneath the bandages. He met his share of disappointing mummies including one which, resisting "hammers, knives and chisels", had to be abandoned, denying the audience their entertainment. The uncertainty was, however, part of the attraction, and his series of six lectures culminating in the unrolling of a mummy – the best tickets one guinea, ladies admitted – were highly popular. London was enthralled by mummy fever.

Pettigrew was no mere entertainer. He took detailed notes as he worked, and in 1834 he published his *History of Egyptian Mummies*, beautifully illustrated by George Cruikshank, illustrator to Charles Dickens. Although Pettigrew was not entirely certain of the ancient embalming process, he subdivided his subjects into those with ventral incisions (both those preserved by balsamic matter

BELOW: BELZONI, MASTER OF PUBLICITY, TURNED PUBLIC "UNROLLINGS" OF MUMMIES INTO POPULAR ENTERTAINMENT.

and those preserved by natron) and those without incisions (those which were salted and filled with bituminous matter, and those which were simply salted). It is clear that the mummies were tested to destruction in order to define their properties:

> *They [the mummies without incisions, salted and filled with bitumen] are black, dry, heavy, and of disagreeable odour, and very difficult to break. Neither the eyebrows nor hair are preserved, and there is no gilding upon them. The bituminous matter is fatty to the touch … and yields a very strong odour. It dissolves imperfectly in alcohol, and when thrown upon hot coals emits a thick smoke and disagreeable smell. When distilled, it gives an abundant oil; fat, and of a brown colour and foetid odour. Exposed to the air, these mummies soon change, attract humidity, and become covered with an efflorescence of saline substances.*

MODERN MUMMIES

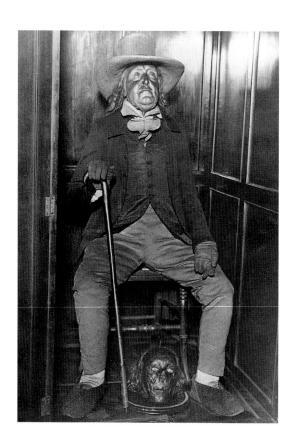

RIGHT: JEREMY BENTHAM, WHOSE MUMMIFIED HEAD LIES BETWEEN THE FEET OF HIS AUTO-ICON AT UNIVERSITY COLLEGE, LONDON.

So great was Dr Pettigrew's fame, and so intense the interest aroused by his public unrollings, that eventually the eccentric Duke of Hamilton approached him with an unusual request. His Grace asked that – after his death – Pettigrew should mummify him, Egyptian style. This was duly done, and the bandaged duke went to his grave in an Egyptian sarcophagus with Pettigrew acting as his priest.

The Duke of Hamilton was not the only Englishman interested in the preservation of the body. On June 6, 1832, Jeremy Bentham died, having left precise instructions concerning the disposal of his remains. Bentham had left his body to medical science – a remarkable decision, given the general distrust of the dissecting room at this time – but he insisted that the dissection be performed in public. Tickets were issued and, in an unusual variant on Pettigrew's well-established lecture-plus-unrolling routine, Dr Southwood Smith gave a talk before cutting up the corpse.

Later Bentham's head was desiccated, his skeleton was articulated and topped with a wax portrait head, and his stuffed clothed body was displayed in a glass case. Bentham's unique "auto-icon" may still be seen in University College, London.

Almost a century later experiments with embalming continued. In Moscow the decision to preserve and display Lenin, who died in 1924, seems to have been influenced by the recent discovery of the mummified Tutankhamen. It was even rumoured that the fluid used to conserve Lenin was based on the ancient Egyptian formula. Flinders Petrie's 1942 deathbed request that his head be preserved was not, however, a result of his lifelong study of Egyptology. Petrie had a great interest in the working of the brain and he hoped that medical science would benefit from his gift.

More recent attempts to mummify a human corpse in the Egyptian style have met with difficulties. The experimental embalming of a human body is the logical reversal of the unrolling of a mummy.

Conducting such an experiment would presumably highlight the inadequacies and flaws in our present knowledge of the technique. However, although the mummification of animals in the name of science is generally considered acceptable (assuming the animal died naturally), there are moral and hygiene implications implicit in the similar treatment of a human body. Can a modern corpse which has been dedicated to scientific research really be used in this way? The distinction between the treatment acceptable for a long-dead corpse and that appropriate to a recently-dead body seems very clear to many.

Dr Bob Brier's attempt to mummify a human cadaver in strict Egyptian style – including the seventy-day drying period in a guarded open tent – on the campus of Long Island University was met with a horrified refusal from the college authorities. The embalming eventually went ahead during the summer of 1994 at the University of Maryland's School of Medicine, using natron and spices obtained from Egypt.

MODERN UNROLLINGS

Unwrappings continued, gradually becoming less of a public spectacle and more of a scientific operation. It was now widely recognized that mummies could be more than simple curiosities. The mummy was a ready packaged source of data capable of yielding important information about both the individual and his or her environment.

Unwrappings, properly conducted and recorded, would aid research.

However, particularly when conducted by Egyptologists rather than by surgeons or physical anthropologists, unwrappings could still be both swift and brutal. All too often little or no interest was shown in either the technique used to bandage

BELOW: THE MUMMIFIED HEAD OF RAMESSES II.

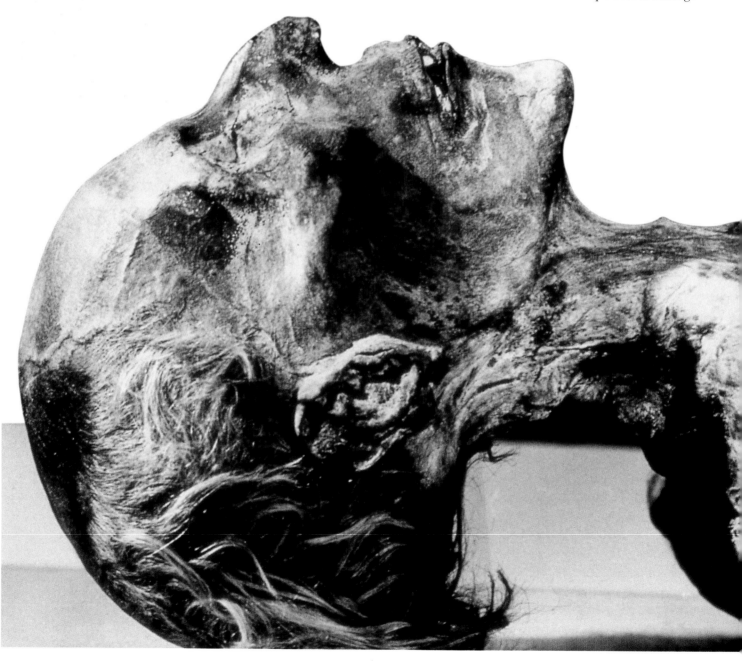

the corpse or the method of mummification. The Egyptologists were eager to gaze upon the faces of the deceased, and to discover their hidden ornaments, but they lacked the medical knowledge necessary to make an adequate interpretation of their dissection.

In 1886, it took just fifteen minutes for Gaston Maspero, then Director of the Egyptian Antiquities Service, to strip Ramesses II of his bandages, the ancient cloth being slit open with a knife to expose the bones and tissue beneath. Nor was this speed unusual; twenty one of the mummies recovered from the Deir el-Bahari cache were unwrapped within a month.

Twenty years later a more detailed examination of the Cairo remains was conducted by Grafton Elliot Smith, Professor of Anatomy at Cairo and later Dean of the Manchester Medical School. Elliot Smith was able to examine those mummies which had already been unwrapped and was given permission to conduct a few unrollings of his own, although he was not allowed to dissect any of the bodies. Unfortunately, the thick resin which coated many of the bones and the ill treatment which the remains had received since their recovery and initial exposure, severely limited the

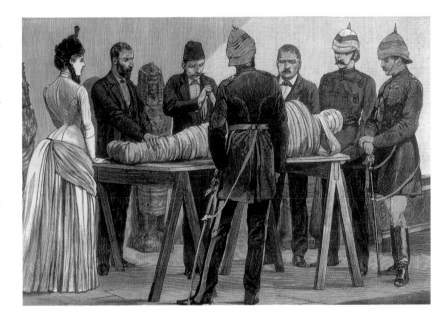

ABOVE: GASTON MASPERO UNWRAPS A MUMMY IN THE CAIRO MUSEUM.

information which Elliot Smith was able to extract. By considering the size and condition of the bones and teeth he was able to suggest ages at, and possible causes of, death. In 1912, Elliot Smith published his catalogue of the royal mummies in Cairo Museum; a volume which provided surprisingly brief descriptions of the human remains, but clear photographs which would prove invaluable in tracing the deterioration of the bodies over the coming years.

RESTORING RAMESSES

Once stripped of their wrappings, little attention was paid to the bodies of the kings. The mummies were simply rewrapped in their original bandages – as far as was possible – and replaced in their coffins. Little or no attempt was made to preserve their remains and the exposed bodies soon started to deteriorate within their display cases.

This neglect seems to be a direct result of the ill-defined status of the museum mummy. Are mummies objects, to be conserved and displayed as any other museum artifact? Or are they human remains which should, as far as is possible, be left to lie in peace? Tutankhamen, lying alone in the Valley of the Kings, fared particularly badly.

Howard Carter, who spent a great deal of his time and energy conserving the numerous artifacts found within the tomb, was not particularly interested in the king's body. Tutankhamen's autopsy was conducted hastily and under far from ideal conditions within the cramped tomb. When it was over it proved very difficult to restore the body to its former condition before returning it to the outermost coffin and sarcophagus. Here the body rested, protected from the public gaze, for more than forty years.

In 1968, Professor Harrison of Liverpool University was given permission to X-ray Tutankhamen's mummy, something which had not

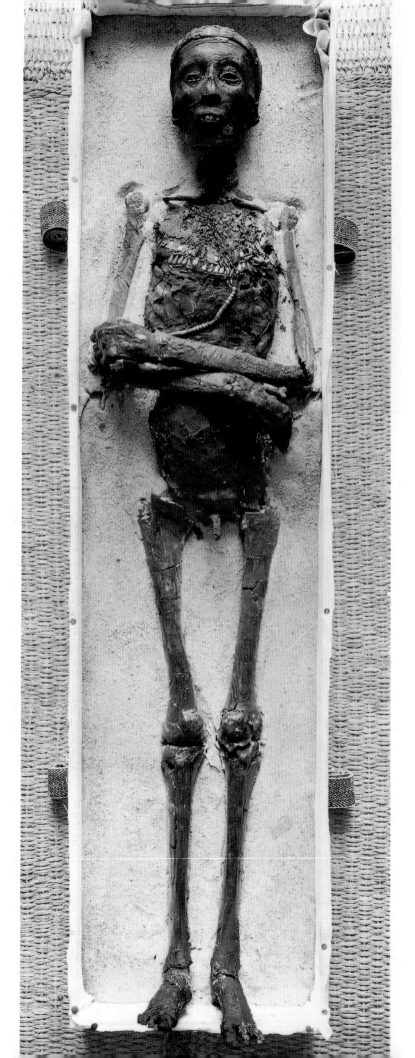

been possible when the body was first discovered. Opening the coffin Professor Harrison discovered that the king's body had never been rewrapped by Carter's team. Tutankhamen was lying naked and dismembered on a simple tray of sand. In order to free the mummy from its coffin and mask, the body had been decapitated and the limbs cut off. Now the king's penis, clearly visible in the earliest photographs, had vanished.

It is always easy to criticize with the benefit of hindsight. Carter and his team were working under very difficult conditions, and both science and the ethics of science have progressed a long was since the 1920s. The mortal remains, and dignity, of a long-dead boy may not have seemed particularly important to a generation hardened by the horrors of the World War One. Carter would almost certainly argue that the mummy, treated with appropriate respect at all times, was nevertheless an artifact to be studied in the best way possible.

And yet it seems a shame that Tutankhamen, for so long intact, had to be dismembered by the very archaeologists who set out to liberate him from obscurity. Harrison's discovery sparked a fierce debate over the natural condition of the body. Had the king really suffered from spontaneous combustion within his coffins? Or did the fact that Carter was compelled to use heat to prize the mummy from his mask have anything to do with the king's carbonized state?

Ramesses II, so badly treated by Maspero and now gradually falling apart, was eventually to be the subject of an extensive restoration programme. In 1975, he was flown in his wooden coffin to the Musée de l'Homme, Paris, where a team of specialists had been assembled to stabilize and improve his condition. Ramesses travelled in style, as befitted a king, with a guard of honour provided at Cairo and Paris airports. It is rumoured that he was even issued with a passport giving his occupation as "king (deceased)".

LEFT: STRIPPED OF ITS COFFINS AND BANDAGES, THE BODY OF THE BOY-KING TUTANKHAMEN APPEARS AS A SMALL AND PATHETIC FIGURE.

RIGHT: AN X-RAY SHOWING THE HEAD OF THE MAJESTIC PHARAOH RAMESSES II

Ramesses, his coffin and wrappings proved to be contaminated with bacteria and almost a hundred species of fungi which were slowly eating him away. It was clearly necessary to sterilize the body to save it. The standard chemical, heating and freezing treatments could have caused incalculable damage to the mummy, therefore the decision was taken to sterilize Ramesses using gamma-rays – a treatment which had previously been used to irradiate precious works of art. Free from all contamination, Ramesses was finally rewrapped in his now clean linen bandages, replaced in his coffin and carefully stored in a specially designed anti-bacterial case.

While Ramesses was undergoing treatment, scientists were able to perform a series of tests on his mummy. X-ray analysis revealed severe arthritis in both hips, arteriosclerosis of the major arteries of the lower limbs and badly worn and abscessed teeth. A sample of Ramesses' silky hair was then analysed. As the pharaoh was over ninety years old

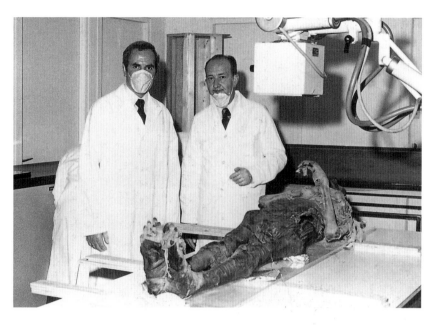

when he died, it came as no surprise to anyone that his natural hair colour was white; the chemicals used to preserve the body had dyed his hair a youthful yellow-red. Analysis of the roots showed that his original hair colour was reddish brown.

ABOVE: RAMESSES II UNDERGOES EXTENSIVE TREATMENT AT THE MUSÉE DE L'HOMME, PARIS.

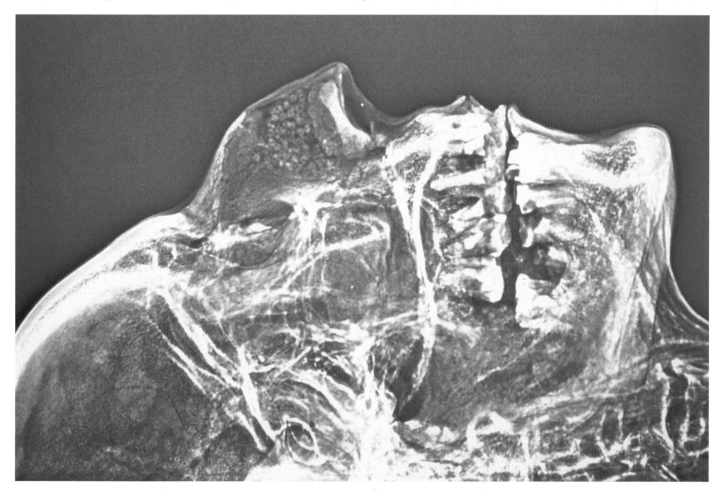

NON-INVASIVE INVESTIGATION

BELOW: X-RAY ANALYSIS OFFERS A NON-DESTRUCTIVE METHOD OF IDENTIFYING AMULETS BENEATH THE MUMMY WRAPPINGS.

FAR BELOW: AN X-RAY OF RAMESSES II CLEARLY CONFIRMS THAT THE KING SUFFERED BADLY FROM ARTHRITIS IN HIS HIP JOINT.

Unwrapping a mummy essentially destroys it, often with little or no scientific advance. The search was on to find a non-destructive means of examining mummies.

The 1895 discovery of X-rays offered the perfect solution. X-ray analysis would allow Egyptologists to see through the layers of bandages, identifying bones and amulets, diseases, age and possible causes of death, without disturbing or damaging the mummy or its wrappings. Although the early X-ray equipment was cumbersome, and it was not at first possible to

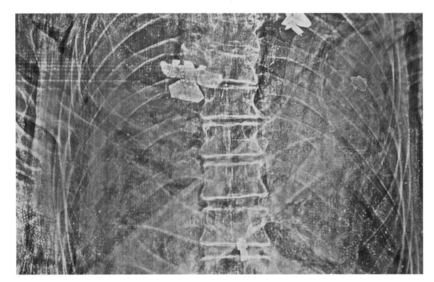

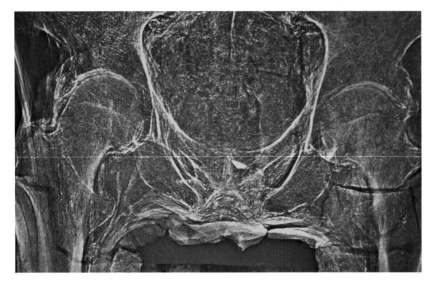

X-ray an entire body, Flinders Petrie, supervising one of the earliest mummy X-rays in 1898, was delighted with what he saw. Soon after the mummy of Tuthmosis IV was X-rayed in an attempt to determine the cause of the king's death. In 1903, there was only one X-ray machine in Cairo and so Tuthmosis, escorted by Elliot Smith, had to make the journey from the museum to a private nursing home by horse-drawn cab. Here he was X-rayed by Dr Khayat. The resulting X-ray helped Elliot Smith to fix the age of the king at death at a relatively young 28 years.

This led to a spate of taking X-rays in various countries, culminating in 1967 with the X-rays of all the royal mummies in Cairo Museum by a team from the University of Michigan School of Dentistry working with Alexandria University. This investigation produced some interesting results, and led to great debate over the age at death of some of the mummies in the Cairo collection.

It is now generally accepted that, although X-ray analysis can be very useful in giving a general indication of mummy age, the dates thus obtained do need to be treated with a degree of caution. An estimated age at death of 35–40 years for the body identified as King Tuthmosis III, for example, cannot possibly be correct, as Tuthmosis is known to have ruled for more than fifty years. The results of the analysis called into question the correct identity of some of the royal mummies recovered from the Deir el-Bahari cache.

X-rays confirmed what earlier unrollings had suggested. Frequently the neat bandages concealed a disarticulated jumble of bones indicative of an advance stage of decay at the time of embalming. Some mummies were wrapped with limbs missing, others were given additional or false ones. The Late Period Lady Teshat, now housed in the Minneapolis Institute of Arts, was even buried with two heads; X-ray analysis of her mummy has revealed a second adult skull tucked between her legs. It would appear that Teshat's mummy had been torn apart in antiquity by robbers. Those responsible for her rewrapping had taken the opportunity to slip the remains of a second, even more damaged mummy into her bandages.

Some embalmers and rewrappers had clearly struggled to prepare the deceased for the Afterlife. One unfortunate New Kingdom lady had to be provided with false viscera; her new liver was made from animal hide and her intestines from a piece of rope. Ramesses VI, hacked apart by tomb robbers, had a piece of his coffin incorporated into his wrappings, while the unfortunate Tuthmosis III

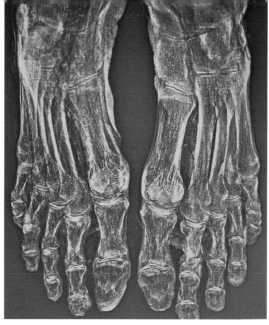

LEFT: THE FEET OF RAMESSES II.

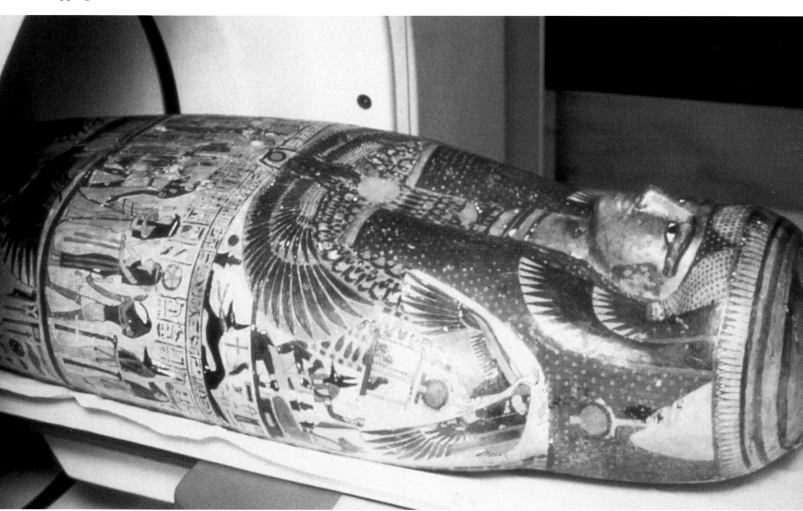

was eventually held together with wooden stiffening. Princess Sitamen, daughter and wife of Amenhotep III was, when unwrapped, represented by a skull, a few bones and three sticks which formed her body. Even the animal mummies were not as they should be; many cat mummies have been found to contain only rags and stuffing while

fake crocodile mummies were cleverly constructed from reeds and the odd bone.

X-ray analysis allowed Egyptologists to take a horizontal, two-dimensional view of the hard tissues through the wrapped body. In the mid 1960s the then new technique of CAT (Computed Axial Tomography) scanning was first used to

ABOVE: A MUMMY FROM THE BRITISH MUSEUM COLLECTION ENTERS THE CAT MACHINE.

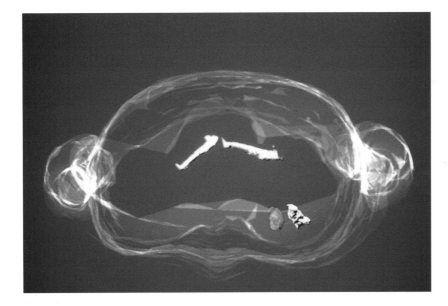

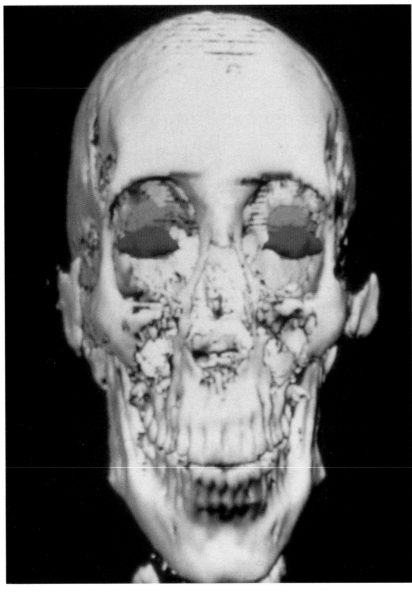

provide a vertical slice through the mummy. The slices could be manipulated by computer to provide a three-dimensional image of the whole body. This visual allowed the scientists to study the remaining soft tissues.

Endoscopy is another development in modern medicine which has been successfully transferred to mummy studies. The endoscope – a long narrow fibre-optic tube tipped with a minute camera – is inserted into the body either through a cut in the skin or via a natural orifice, and pushed into position. Soft tissue can then be examined with the aid of the camera, and small samples can be taken as required. "Soft tissue" is perhaps something of a misnomer when studying mummies. Much of the ancient tissue has hardened with age and the application of resin, making it frequently difficult to insert an endoscope. The technique, although undeniably invasive, is essentially a non-destructive method of sample collection; there is no need to disturb the mummy wrappings in order to view the stomach. The use of endoscopy is now allowing the Manchester Museum to build an impressive mummy tissue collection which may prove useful in the study of mummy DNA.

In 1898, J Kollman and W Buchly published details of the thickness of the soft tissue overlying twenty three defined points on the human skull. This pioneering work led to the development of three-dimensional facial reconstructions which have proved very helpful to the police in the identification of decomposed bodies. The same technique has been used to reconstruct the heads and faces of Egyptian mummies. The original method involved taking a cast of the defleshed head. Modelling clay could then be used to build up layers of soft tissue of appropriate thickness guided by aluminium posts of predetermined length screwed into the cast. Finally, individual features, such as wrinkles, could be guessed and added. Today's computer analysis and CAT scans make it possible to reconstruct the features without removing either the skin or the bandages from the skull.

ABOVE LEFT: CAT SCANNING HAS PRODUCED SOME UNEXPECTED RESULTS; HERE, FOR EXAMPLE, SHABTI FIGURES WERE FOUND IN THE STOMACH OF THIS 21ST-DYNASTY MUMMY.
LEFT: THE SKULL OF THE SAME MUMMY REVEALED BY A CAT SCAN; THE PINK AREAS INDICATE FALSE EYES.

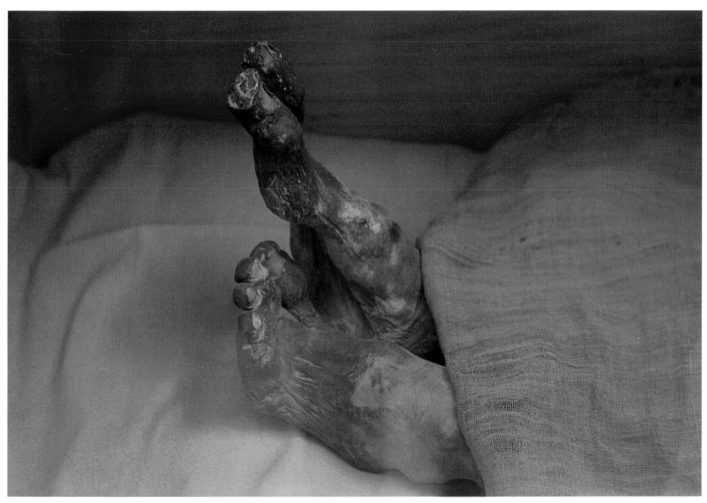

 # THE HEALTHY MUMMY

ABOVE: THE DEFORMED LEFT
LEG OF KING SIPTAH WAS
PROBABLY THE RESULT OF
CEREBRAL PALSY OR POLIO.

Many of the mummies subjected to X-ray analysis have revealed the unmistakable marks of violence. Fractures and head wounds are commonly found in those who served as soldiers, providing a reminder of the harsh realities of the ancient battlefield. Occasionally, the veteran campaigner may be identified by his healed wounds; in addition to the fatal blows which killed him, King Sekenere Tao also had a partially healed cut above his ear. However, not all mummy wounds were inflicted before death. The knife or axe wounds on the body of King Merenptah, for example, were almost certainly caused by thieves who damaged his shoulder, cut open his stomach and pulled off his right arm in a frantic search for concealed jewellery and other valuables.

The survival of many mummies with substantial quantities of soft tissue intact has allowed scientists to learn more about the health and living conditions of the ancient Egyptians than has been possible for other past civilizations. Occasionally, it is easy to diagnose the ancient ailments; the mummy of Ramesses V still shows the diagnostic smallpox pustules which killed the king. Others are less clear; King Siptah's deformed left leg has been variously classified as polio, cerebral palsy and club foot.

It is now possible to rehydrate mummy tissue, allowing scientists to cut the thin sections needed for microscopic examination. Some mummies have even yielded DNA samples. Cloning from rehydrated mummy DNA is now theoretically possible, although the rather sinister image of the mad professor resurrecting a long-dead mummy from its coffin remains firmly in the realm of science fiction. It is hoped that, given time, this line of research may eventually help establish the royal family trees of Egypt.

Many mummies show signs of parasitic infestation which, if not life threatening, must have made life very uncomfortable for their hosts. Tape worms, Guinea worms – lengthy worms which can cause intense discomfort before emerging through a sore on the leg – and strongyl worms, which enter the host via the feet and migrate to the lungs and throat causing asthma-like symptoms – plagued the population. Evidence of mosquito-born malaria has been obtained from immunological tests conducted on rehydrated mummy tissue. Bilharzia, still a problem in modern Egypt, was widespread; sufferers experienced swelling of the genitalia and blood in the urine.

The bilharzia worm lives in the slow-moving waters at the edge of the River Nile and in the irrigation canals. Entering the human host it attaches itself to the walls of the blood vessels so that its eggs pass into the blood supply. The eggs

then move into the bladder or bowel and make their way out of the host. Entering stagnant water they hatch into larvae and spend some time in an intermediate host – a water snail – before passing again into the water and repeating the entire cycle. This disease has been found in predynastic sand-dried mummies and is most common in the fishermen, farmers, laundrymen and housewives who would have spent much of their working day wading in shallow water.

If parasites troubled the living, then miniature scavengers preyed on the dead. It would have been virtually impossible to keep insects away from the decomposing corpses, and flies and their pupa are commonly found within mummy bandages. Carrion beetles were a definite menace in the embalming house. Once they had become incorporated within the mummy wrappings they were quite capable of laying eggs, hatching, feasting off skin and tissue, mating and dying without ever seeing the light of day. One mummy unwrapped by Pettigrew had over 270 carrion beetles in its skull. The only hope of avoiding infestation was to get the body to the undertakers as quickly as possible.

BELOW: THE TEETH CAN REVEAL MUCH ABOUT THE LIFE OF A MUMMY; ELDERLY EGYPTIANS INVARIABLY SUFFERED FROM DENTAL ATTRITION – AN INEVITABLE CONSEQUENCE OF THEIR GRIT-FILLED DIET.

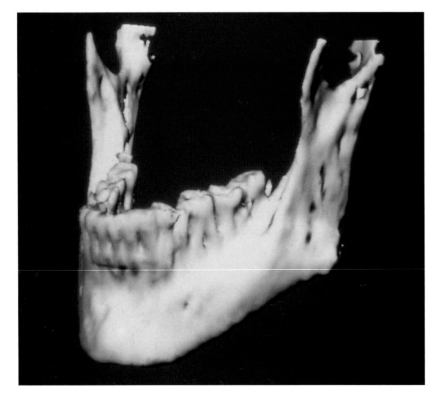

TEETH

Teeth, usually the best preserved part of any corpse or skeleton, form a highly specialized branch of mummy studies. Teeth can provide information on age, health, diet and even family resemblances; we now know, for example, that the mummies of the late 17th to early 18th Dynasty queens Tetisheri (great grandmother), Ahmose Nefertari (mother) and Ahmose (daughter) all had remarkably prominent bucked teeth in their similar-shaped heads.

The unfortunate Egyptians suffered greatly from toothache. Decay, or caries, caused by excessive sugar consumption, was a disease limited to the wealthy. Sugar was only available in the form of honey and this was a luxury beyond the reach of most Egyptians. However, the standard daily diet was high in bread made from stone-ground cereal that incorporated a large quantity of wind-blown sand. This eroded the teeth and gradually wore them down to the gums. This extensive wear on the teeth of adult Egyptians can make it hard to estimate age of death on the basis of teeth alone.

Many mummies show signs of dental abscesses; Amenhotep III was a typical sufferer. When Elliot Smith examined the king's decayed and tartar-coated teeth he noted that "during the last years of his life Amenothes [Amenhotep] II must have suffered most acutely from tooth-ache". The Egyptian doctors had no real understanding of dentistry and could do nothing to stop the pain. Religion offered little help; Amenhotep's dedication of 600 statues to the goddess Sekhmet brought him no relief and he was forced to write to his brother-in-law, King Tushratta of Mittani, asking if he could borrow the famous healing statue of Ishtar. This too seems to have failed, as the king died soon after the statue arrived in Egypt. Continuous toothache undermined the general health of the sufferer, while badly infected teeth, in the absence of antibiotics, could kill.

LEFT: THIS CT RECONSTRUCTION OF A MUMMY'S TEETH SHOWS EVIDENCE OF AN EARLY DEATH.

The ubiquitous desert sand had an adverse effect on the lungs. Frequent inhalation of sand and dust led to sand pneumoconiosis or silicosis – a constant scourge of desert dwellers. The lungs of many mummies show a high silica content.

Smoke inhalation from fires and oil lamps burning in an enclosed environment rather than from tobacco (which was unknown to the ancient Mediterranean world), could also prove hazardous to health, leaving a debilitating sooty deposit on the lungs.

BENEATH THE BANDAGES

Recently there has been a renewed interest in the unwrapping of mummies as an aid to scientific investigation. These unwrappings are far removed from the public entertainments of the Victorian age. Often they are undertaken as a last resort, when the body's deteriorating condition makes disposal the only realistic alternative. The mummies are at all times treated with the respect due to a deceased human being. The unwrapping is carried out slowly under scientific conditions by a multi-disciplinary team of archaeologists and medics. Every aspect of the body and its covering is studied in minute detail using modern techniques of histology, microscopy, chemical analysis and microbiology. The remains are then retained for future study. The information obtained in this way can prove invaluable.

One of the earliest mummies to be unwrapped under modern scientific conditions was "Melvin", a mummy from the collection of Brooklyn Museum. Melvin had been purchased by accident in the 1950s; the museum had wanted to buy his cartonnage mummy case, but not Melvin himself. Attempts to dispose of the unwanted mummy failed miserably. As Melvin did not have a death certificate, the police refused permission to bury the corpse in the museum garden. It was not possible to sell Melvin to a neighbouring museum either; without a death certificate no corpse could legally pass the state line. The decision was therefore taken to unwrap the mummy, and Melvin became a minor media celebrity. Today he remains on display in Brooklyn Museum.

 # THE MANCHESTER MUMMY

ABOVE: DR MARGARET MURRAY (SECOND FROM RIGHT) OVERSEEING THE SCIENTIFIC UNWRAPPING OF ONE OF THE 12TH DYNASTY "TWO BROTHERS" AT MANCHESTER MUSEUM.

In 1975 a Roman-style female mummy in the collection of Manchester Museum, known simply as "mummy 1770", was unwrapped by a team of specialists led by Egyptologist Dr Rosalie David. This mummy was of uncertain provenance, but was thought to have come from the Hawara cemetery in the Faiyum. Manchester Museum already had a reputation for unrolling mummies. In 1906 Dr Margaret Murray had unwrapped the "Two Brothers", two mummies recovered from a 12th

Dynasty tomb at Rifeh. Dr Murray's explorations were not particularly informative but tissue samples taken in the course of her work were re-studied in the 1970s, revealing the unmistakable signs of silicosis of the lungs.

X-ray analysis indicated that all might not be as expected beneath the wrappings of 1770. The body was that of a young girl, about 15 years of age. It was clear that her lower legs had suffered exten-sive damage. The left leg was broken below the knee, the right leg above the knee and both feet were missing. In addition there was a curious compact bundle between the thighs. When unrolled this package was found to contain a pair of false feet, which would have enabled the deceased to walk in the Afterlife. The legs appeared to have been broken after death, and the undertakers had attempted to make good the damage by supplying the young girl with artificial legs. Peculiarly, the young girl had been provided with nipple shields and an artificial penis.

The skull bore traces of paint, indicating that the body had been at least partially decomposed before wrapping. Speculation was rife. Had the girl fallen into the Nile, and been part-eaten by a crocodile? Radio-carbon dating eventually suggested an answer to the puzzle. Although the wrappings belonged to the Roman Period, the bones within might well be considerably older. It seems that the body had been mummified, opened (by thieves?) and rewrapped at a time when putrefaction had already set in. The embalmers, unable to determine the sex of the body, thoughtfully provided it with both male and female private parts.

Why should the embalmers go to so much trouble and expense to preserve the remains of an unknown non-royal girl? As yet, we do not know but it is possible that the crocodile theory should not be totally discarded. Throughout the Ptolemaic period those who were attacked by crocodiles were accorded special respect. This invariably included an elaborate burial.

THE BRISTOL MUMMY

BELOW: THE BRISTOL MUSEUM MUMMY PROJECT SET NEW STANDARDS IN SCIENTIFIC MUMMY ANALYSIS.

The mummy of Horemkenesi, a minor priest of the 21st Dynasty, was recovered from a rock-cut tomb during the 1904-5 season of excavations at Deir el-Bahari conducted by the Egypt Exploration Society. As part of the British share of the finds the mummy was sent to the Egypt Exploration Society in London and thence to Bristol Museum, where it was catalogued as HA7386. Already its condition was giving some cause for concern. However the mummy remained stable until the unusually hot summer of 1976 when it started to show unmistakable signs of decomposition. Soon there were holes in the bandages and a thin layer of salt covering the body. The decision was therefore taken to unwrap the mummy before it fell apart.

The Bristol mummy was unwrapped in 1981 in the Department of Anatomy, Bristol University. David Dawson, Curator of the Museum, headed a multi-disciplinary team which followed many of the procedures established by the Manchester mummy team some six years earlier. As is now standard procedure, the unwrapping started with X-ray analysis. The unwrapping – which lasted for

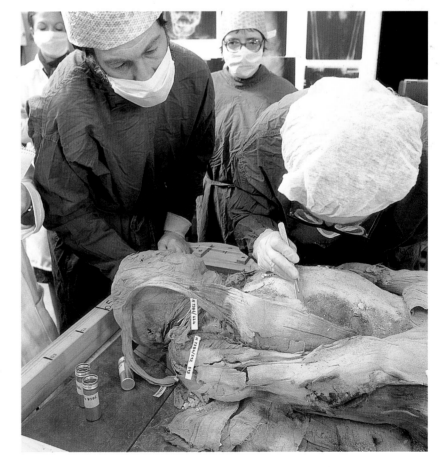

two weeks – was then followed by a full autopsy and many samples were retained for future study.

Once again, the team had chosen a mummy with an unusual history. As the unwrapping progressed it became clear that the inner wrappings, but not the outer ones, were heavily contaminated with carrion beetle. This indicated that the body had become infested some time before the preliminary wrapping was completed. The face, arms, legs and feet of the mummy all showed extensive beetle damage and there were numerous insect holes through the cheek and the neck. Beneath the bandages the mummy was in poor condition.

Most unusually, although the body had been fully eviscerated, the brain had been left in place only to decay and be eaten by insects within the skull. In contrast the heart had been removed. The internal organs were unfortunately missing; in a mummy of this age they would normally have been preserved within the wrappings.

Horemkenesi was revealed to have died a plump, elderly, clean-shaven man with a slightly deformed nose and bad teeth. He had suffered from both bilharzia and malaria. The lack of internal organs made it difficult to speculate on the cause of his death but, given that his body had apparently been infected by beetles before it reached the undertakers, pathologist Norman Brown suggested that Horemkenesi may have suffered a fatal heart attack or stroke while away from home. The time that it took to find his body would be enough, in the heat of the Egyptian sun, for nature to take her course. The undertakers would have seen little point in extracting the already rotten brain, while the viscera may have been too decomposed to preserve.

One very unusual feature of the Bristol project was the decision to allow the general public to watch the unwrapping and autopsy by means of closed-circuit television. At first this may seem like a throwback to the morbid public entertainments of the Victorian age. However, the atmosphere throughout the Bristol experiment was very different from that at Dr Pettigrew's celebrated unrollings. The Bristol team took the decision to broadcast the unwrapping after considering the great public interest which the project had aroused. Care was taken at all times to ensure the body was treated with the proper respect.

THE MYSTERIOUS OCCUPANT OF TOMB 55

Modern scientific analysis has gone a long way towards explaining one of the greatest mysteries of mummy studies: the unnamed body recovered from Tomb 55 in the Valley of the Kings.

The sequence of events towards the end of the Amarna Period – the time when the heretic king Akhenaten served the single god Aten from his new capital city Akhetaten – now seems very blurred. We know that Akhenaten was married to Queen Nefertiti, by whom he had six daughters. As far as we are aware, Nefertiti never bore a son. However, Akhenaten, like all pharaohs, enjoyed a harem full of secondary wives and one of these, the Lady Kiya, was his particular favourite. It seems that Kiya bore Akhenaten at least one, and probably two sons.

The young Tutankhamen came to the throne four or five years after the death of Akhenaten. But who was Tutankhamen? Who were his parents, and who ruled in the period between Akhenaten and Tutankhamen? Smenkhkare, an ephemeral figure, has been identified as the missing king. Some believed Smenkhkare to be the brother or son of Akhenaten. Others felt that Smenkhkare was the throne name of Nefertiti, who had succeeded her husband to rule as a king.

Tomb 55, a simple grave consisting of a sloping passage and a single burial chamber, was discovered in 1907 by a team of archaeologists working for Theodore Davis. The excavators found the burial chamber in a complete mess, with a confusing mixture of grave goods and refuse scattered all over the floor. However, there was no sign of a break-in and the mummy still lay intact within its coffin. The ownership of the tomb was far from clear: the grave goods included the names of various late 18th Dynasty kings ranging from Amenhotep II to Tutankhamen. All that could be determined was that the tomb could not have been sealed before Tutankhamen acceded to the throne.

There was no sarcophagus – which was perhaps a sign that the tomb had been needed in a hurry – but there were four canopic jars discovered in a niche in the chamber wall. The coffin itself was badly damaged. It had been laid to rest on a wooden bed but this had collapsed, sending the coffin crashing to the floor. As the coffin lid had come loose in the fall, the mummy, now lying in a puddle of water, started to rot. Further damage was caused when a rock fell from the roof and split the coffin in two. By the time it was removed from the tomb the coffin was in fragments; it was later reconstructed at Cairo Museum where it proved to be made of gilded wood inlaid with semi-precious stones.

The head of the anthropoid coffin wore a wig rather than a crown. This indicated that it had not been designed for a king. However, soon after its manufacture, the coffin had been fitted with the beard and uraeus – cobra – which made it suitable for the interment of a royal male. After the burial both the uraeus and the gold face-mask had been ripped away, leaving the wood of the coffin exposed. The measurements and design of the coffin showed that it had been built for a woman and indeed the texts which decorated its surface were intended to be spoken by a woman – someone who could be described as the beloved of Pharaoh Akhenaten.

LEFT: AKHENATEN AND HIS QUEEN, NEFERTITI WORSHIP A SOLAR DISC.

**RIGHT: A STATUE OF
AKHENATEN AND HIS QUEEN**

Again, before the coffin was used, these inscriptions had been altered from feminine to masculine and the name of the original owner had been replaced by a name in a royal cartouche, which was itself later erased.

A series of fragile gilded and inscribed wooden panels found in the corridor and burial chamber proved to be parts of a shrine made by Akhenaten for the funeral of his mother, Queen Tiy. The four canopic jars were equally puzzling. They, too, had been labelled and then erased, leaving the jars anonymous. Recent analysis has proved that they were made for Kiya, although the lids of the jars – four beautifully carved female heads – are so ill-

fitting that they may not be the original stoppers. The contents of three of the jars were sent for analysis, with two yielding a "hard, compact, black, pitch-like mass surrounding a well-defined centrally-situated zone of different material, which was of a brown colour and friable nature".

What conclusions could the excavators draw from this tangled web of evidence? The shrine obviously belonged to Queen Tiy and so, Theodore Davis assumed, did the coffin and the mummy. However, the coffin bore the titles of King Akhenaten, albeit with his name erased. The gold bands found within the mummy wrappings also bore Akhenaten's name, but these were stolen before they could be properly recorded. Maybe those who buried the mummy believed that they were burying the king himself?

Who lay in the anthropoid coffin? To this day, archaeologists cannot agree. Theodore Davis and Arthur Weigall were among those present as the unrolling began, and Davis later published his account of the operation:

> Presently, we cleared the mummy from the
> coffin, and found that it was a smallish
> person, with a delicate head and hands.
> The mouth was partly open, showing a
> perfect set of upper and lower teeth.
> The body was enclosed in mummy-cloth
> of fine texture, but all of the cloth covering
> the body was of a very dark colour …
> Rather suspecting injury from the evident
> dampness, I gently touched one of the
> front teeth (3,000 years old) and alas! it
> fell into dust, thereby showing that the
> mummy could not be preserved …

Davis could be heavy-handed when dealing with mummies – he once famously tested the strength of a mummy's hair by pulling it – but in this case it seems that the body was already damaged beyond repair. The water which, over the centuries, had dripped into the tomb had wreaked havoc and the mummy disintegrated as soon as it was touched. Joseph Lindon Smith, the artist who unrolled the mummy, later described how it eerily "crumbled into ashes and sifted down through

ACKNOWLEDGEMENTS

The publishers would like to thank the following sources for their kind permission to reproduce the pictures in this book:

AKG London 12, 20l, 30, 38, 43, 92/Erich Lessing 6, 9, 14, 15, 21, 22, 24, 27, 28t, 32, 35tl, 36, 39, 44tl, 45, 46bl

Bridgeman Art Library, London/New York /British Museum, London *Eye of Horus,* amulet to protect health and fortune, late Dynastic period, c.600 BC, 28b/Egyptian mummy of a Priestess, 21st Dynasty, 1085–935 BC, 31br /Ibis-headed Thoth, Judge of the Dead, relief carving, Ancient Egyptian, 66 /**Freud Museum, London** Human-headed Ba bird, Egyptian, Ptolemaic period 332–30 BC, 20 r /Mummified falcon, representing the funerary deity Sokar, lord of Rostau, Egyptian late period, 716–332 BC, 65 /**Giraudon, Louvre, Paris** *The Liberation of the Dead,* detail from the interior of the sarcophagus of Amenemipet, a priest of the cult of Amenophis (Amenhotep) I, Thebes, 16th Century BC (painted plaster on wood), 42 /**Louvre, Paris** Egyptian statuette of Amenophis IV (Akhenaten) and Nefertiti, Amarna period, 1365–1349 BC 124 /**Museo e Gallerie Nazional di Capodimonte, Naples/Roger Viollet, Paris** *Alexander the Great, from the mosaic of The Battle of Alexander Against the Persians at the Battle of Issus,* 333 BC, from the House of Faun, Pompeii, late 2nd or early 1st century BC after a 4th century BC Hellenistic painting by Philoxenos of Eritrea, 26 /**Peter Willi, Louvre, Paris** Coffin of a cat protected by the God Bastet, Dynastic Era, BC, 68l

Bristol Museums and Art Gallery 121
Christie's Images 83tl
Peter Clayton 16, 49, 51, 52b, 53, 54t, 54br, 55, 59, 60tr, 60bl, 61tr, 61bl, 62, 67bl, 72, 100, 106, 117
Corbis/Bettmann/Reuter, 108/Everett Collection, 101, 102tl, 102bl, 103/Farrell Grehan, 88tl/Roger Wood, 84
Reg Davis 104r, 104l, 110, 113tr, 113b, 114b, 114t, 115b, 115t, 116t, 116b, 118, 119
et archive 10t, 13, 19, 23, 31t, 33, 34, 45br, 47, 48, 63, 67r, 69, 78tl, 78bl, 81, 86, 105, 123
Mary Evans Picture Library 35t, 37, 73, 75tr,

77, 80, 87, 89, 90, 93, 94, 111/Institution of Civil Engineers, 52tl
John Frost 88bl
Hulton Getty 18, 68br, 70, 71, 74, 75bl, 76, 79, 82, 83br, 85, 88c, 91, 108bl, 125
Ronald Grant Archive 96, 98
Griffith Institute, Ashmoleon Museum, Oxford 112
Robert Harding Picture Library 7, 11r, 25, 29, 40, 46tr, 50, 57, 58, 64
Illustrated London News Picture Library 107br
London Features International Ltd/Stephen Trupp 99tr
Manchester Museum, University of Manchester 120
Science Photo Library/Klaus Guldbrandsen 17

Every effort has been made to acknowledge correctly and contact the source and/copyright holder of each picture, and Carlton Books Limited apologises for any unintentional errors or omissions which will be corrected in future editions of this book.

▲

FURTHER READING

ANCIENT EGYPT
Baines, J. and Malek, J. (1980), *Atlas of Ancient Egypt*, New York and Oxford
Belzoni, G.B. (1820), *Narrative of the Operations and Recent Discoveries in Egypt and Nubia*, London.
Kemp, B.J. (1989), *Ancient Egypt: anatomy of a civilization*, London and New York
Romer, J. (1981), *Valley of the Kings*, London.
Reeves, N. and Wilkinson, R.H. (1996*), The Complete Valley of the Kings*, London.

MUMMIFICATION
Andrews, C. (1984), *Egyptian Mummies*, London.
Adams, B (1984), *Egyptian Mummies*, Princes Risborough.
Budge, E.A.W. (1925), *The Mummy: A Handbook of Egyptian Funerary Archaeology*, Cambridge.
Brier, B. (1994), *Egyptian Mummies: Unravelling the Secrets of an Ancient Art*, New York.
El Mahdy, C. (1989), *Mummies, Myths and Magic*, London.

Ikram, S. and Dodson, A. (1998), *The Mummy in Ancient Egypt: Equipping the Dead for Eternity*, London.
Partridge, R.B. (1994), *Faces of Pharaohs: Royal Mummies and Coffins from Ancient Thebes*, London.
Spencer, A.J. (1982), *Death in Ancient Egypt*, London.

TUTANKHAMEN
Carter, H. (1925) *The Tomb of Tutankhamen*, London, 3 volumes; reprinted 1972 in 1 volume.
Desroches-Noblecourt, C. (1963), *Tutankhamen: Life and Death of a Pharaoh*, London and New York.
Hoving, T. (1978), *Tutankhamun: the Untold Story*, New York.
James, T.G.H. (1992), *Howard Carter: The Path to Tutankhamun*, London.
Reeves, N (1990), *The Complete Tutankhamun*, London.

SCIENTIFIC ANALYSIS
Cockburn, A. and E. (1980), *Mummies, Disease and Ancient Cultures*, Cambridge.
David, A.R. ed. (1979), *The Manchester Museum Project*, Manchester.
David, A.R. and Tapp, E. eds (1984), *Evidence Embalmed*, Manchester.
Harris, J.E. and Weeks, K.R. (1973), *X-Raying the Pharaohs*, New York and London.
Pettigrew, T.J. (1834), *A History of Egyptian Mummies*, London.
Smith, G.E. (1912), *The Royal Mummies*, Cairo.
Taylor, J.H. (1995), *Unwrapping a Mummy*, London.

THE MUMMY IN POPULAR CULTURE
Freyling, C. (1992), *The Face of Tutankhamun*, London.
Madison, A. (1980), *Mummies in Fact and Fiction*, London.
Ikram and Dodson (1998), *The Mummy in Ancient Egypt*, give a useful list of "Mummies in the Media" while Brier (1994), *Egyptian Mummies*, includes an interesting chapter on mummies in film.